PASTORAL MUSIC
IN PRACTICE

A Collection of Articles First Published
in Pastoral Music Magazine

Edited by
Rev. Virgil C. Funk and Gabe Huck

A Joint Publication

The Pastoral Press
National Association of Pastoral Musicians
Washington, D.C.

Liturgy Training Publications
Chicago, Illinois

Articles in this publication first appear in *Pastoral Music*, copyrighted 1976, 1977, 1978, 1979.

The Pastoral Press
National Association of Pastoral Musicians
225 Sheridan Street NW, Washington, DC 20011
(202) 723-5800

Liturgy Training Publications
155 East Superior Street, Chicago, IL 60611
(312) 751-8382

ISBN 0-9602378-3-6   All rights reserved.
© The National Association of Pastoral Musicians 1981.

Manufactured in the United States of America

CONTENTS

Introduction. *Rev. Virgil C. Funk.* v

I. THE MINISTRY OF MUSIC

Music Ministry, Today and Tomorrow. *Most Rev. Rembert Weakland, OSB.* 1

The Dilemma of Pastoral Music. *Rev. John Melloh, SM.* 10

The Musician as Minister. *Rev. Nathan Mitchell, OSB.* 20

The Animator. *Rev. Joseph Gelineau, SJ.* 35

II. MUSIC AND OUR PRAYER

The Church as a Community of Prayer. *Rev. Godfrey Diekmann, OSB.* 43

A God Who Hears. *Rev. Nathan Mitchell, OSB.* 55

Six Minor Heresies in Today's Music. *Rev. Nathan Mitchell, OSB.* 69

Two Become One: Performance and Participation. *Rev. Paul Philibert, OP.* 75

III. MUSIC IN THE LITURGY

Choosing Music: No Small Task. *Mr. Tom Conry.* 81

Contents

Setting the Tone. *Rev. Robert Dufford, SJ.* 89

Beyond the Spectator Sacraments. *Mr. Ken Meltz.* 97

Pastoral Liturgy is NOT in the Book. *Mr. Ralph Keifer.* 103

Musical, Liturgical, Pastoral Judgmnts: New Songs, New Judgments? *Rev. William Bauman.* 107

IV. TOOLS AND TASKS

Our People Just Don't Like to Sing. Good Environment Helps. New Music: Step by Step. How the Organist Can Lead the Congregation. *Mr. Robert J. Batastini.* 117

Prayer and Music: Singing the Meaning of the Words. *Rev. Michael Joncas.* 135

Hymns In History. *Dr. Alice Parker.* 141

INTRODUCTION

The musical tradition of the universal Church is a treasure of immeasurable value, greater even than that of any other art. The main reason for this preeminence is that, as sacred melody united to words, it forms a necessary or integral part of the solemn liturgy... Liturgical action is given a more noble form when sacred rites are solemnized in song, with the assistance of sacred ministers and the active participation of the people.
— *Constitution on the Sacred Liturgy*, Nos. 112, 113

With this statement in the *Constitution on the Sacred Liturgy*, promulgated in December 1963, the members of the Second Vatican Council affirmed the integral connection between liturgy and music, as well as the importance of the "sacred ministers" and the assembled congregation. In the years since the Council, we have come to learn just how central these three priciples are: that musical liturgy is normative; that the musician is a key figure in animating the liturgical celebration; and that the whole assembly must assume its responsibility as principal worshiper of the Almighty God. *Pastoral Music in Practice*, a joint publication of the National Association of Pastoral Musicians (NPM) and Liturgy Training Publications (LTP), addresses these three areas of concern. First, a word about the publishers; then a word about the book.

The National Association of Pastoral Musicians is a membership organization of clergy and musicians dedicated to fostering the art of liturgical music. *Pastoral Music*, its membership journal, regularly addresses current issues affecting the pastoral musician and clergy. Liturgy Training Publications, the publishing arm of the Office for Divine Worship, Archdiocese of Chicago, develops resources and publications for training those engaged in liturgical ministry.

Introduction

A need exists for a publication to combine the musical expertise of NPM with the training expertise of LTP. The best articles from the first three years of *Pastoral Music* magazine were selected by an editorial team from LTP and NPM: Dolly Sokol, Mike Tapia and Gina Doggett joined the editors in making the final choices for this book.

Our intention was to select from *Pastoral Music* those pages which could continue to offer to musicians, clergy and others working together in liturgy strong insight and honest inspiration. Notions about the very ministry of music (Section I), the bonds between music and prayer (Section II) and the way our liturgical prayer is naturally musical (Section III) shaped the book and brought us to conclude with practical aspects of implementation (Section IV). But the practical, the theory and the spirit are interwoven in a marvelous way throughout the entire book.

NPM and LTP are happy to join in this venture. LTP presents a high standard of quality in all its publishing (a partial list is given on page 150). NPM remains committed to excellence in musical celebration. Together we hope to present parish practitioners with the finest resources possible.

(Rev.) Vigil C. Funk
President, NPM

Gabe Huck
Director, LTP

PASTORAL MUSIC
IN PRACTICE

I. THE MINISTRY OF MUSIC

MUSIC MINISTRY, TODAY AND TOMORROW

M. Rev. Rembert Weakland, OSB
Archbishop of Milwaukee, musician and liturgist.

To talk to a select group of dedicated church musicians about the importance of the role of music in worship and prayer is like carrying coals to Newscastle or beer to Milwaukee. We are all convinced that it is the other person who is not here who should hear our message. Perhaps we can examine our present position, try to analyze where we are — even what we might be doing wrong — and thus prepare today a better tomorrow.

The analysis revolves around the two questions: *What should liturgical music be like today?* and *What should the liturgical musician be like today?*

Concerning the music itself and its content, it should be the best of music, and nothing but the best. To reiterate such a truism might seem out of place and unnecessary, but we have been slipping too much in our standards. Music in worship must be true art. If we today keep this standard high, we will be preparing in the best way possible for tomorrow.

Now let us apply this truism that we would all accept to some concrete situations. The first that comes to mind is a liturgy in which careful attention and rehearsal has been given to every note the choir is to sing and the poor congregation has to struggle just to make it through, being supported — or more often submerged — by a harsh and overbearing organ. Rarely today do we find a congregation that does not do some singing—if there still are such congregations, then we musicians are to blame—but the quality of the singing is another matter. We must now reach for the second plateau. The congregation must sing well—not just the choir. Often the contrast between the two is so marked that the members of the congregation must feel like crawling under the pews to hide. Surely no choirmaster would gleefully tolerate a situation in which the choir comes off better!

The congregation, too, must find the musical experience genuine and satisfying. People demand more today in terms of performance because they hear and experience so much perfection on television and radio. The days of the amateur hour are over. What is worse than a motet sung to perfection by a choir, followed by a no-one-knows-where-to-begin hymn that is twice as slow as it should be?

The major problem with the people's part is that there is no time to rehearse. Rehearsals before Mass often are not the best preparation for the Mass itself. One can, of course, begin with the school children, gradually introduce a new hymn by letting the choir do it first and have the organist play some improvisations on the tune, but ultimately someone has to take the congregation in hand and give it a bit of discipline. Could it be that we are expecting too big a repertoire of our congregations? Less music—if it is good music well sung—is better than constantly having to face new material for which the first performance is the pre-Mass rehearsal. If it is good music, repetition becomes a delight, not a penance. Perhaps what is needed are shorter, cheaper, better hymnals to help develop a good national repertoire.

It is hoped that we have by now passed the stage of choirs competing with congregations or choirs being dropped as outmoded. At least in Milwaukee the choirs are well and thriving. Normally there is more than one choir: the adult choir that theoretically is number one and does tougher stuff, the youth or folk choir (usually with a few older people happy to be among the youth), the children's choir, and then those volunteers who sacrifice their time to sing at funerals—the deadbeats or Resurrectional choirs. The proficiency of these choirs is amazing. The quality of performance is excellent. The greatest weakness is not so much the quality of the execution as it is the scarcity of a good and flexible repertoire. So often I have the feeling of being served what happened to have been left over in the deep-freeze, rather than what is appropriate and liturgically proper. No doubt the problem of always new and changing texts cannot be easily solved; for this reason, the Middle Ages brought about psalm-tones, the Renaissance *falso bordone*, and the Russian Orthodox those resounding polyphonic chord structures. But I do not want to belabor this point: I am willing and able to eat leftovers as long as we try to create new and suitable music and composers are taking this challenge of the choir and its repertoire seriously.

Before leaving the aspects of performance, however, let me make a resounding plea for better acoustics in our churches and better equipment as well. Having now to say Mass under so many varied circumstances and in so many different churches, I have become acutely aware of this problem. So many new churches are acoustically dead and have a loud-speaking system that must have been invented by the devil to prevent the Word of God from being heard. The tone is often made harsh and unpleasant, or all runs together. The new liturgy presupposes that everyone can hear everything.

If, however, the performance must be the best, so must the quality of the music. We must all be more exacting on the kind or quality of the music being used. If you are a member of the liturgy commission or committee of your parish and all the other members want "You Are My Sunshine" for the Mass of Resurrection, it is your task to remain obstinate for good musical taste. Several years ago we were all a bit lenient, allowing or closing an ear to something a bit second-rate if it only got the people to sing. But now it is time to aim higher. Most important of all is that regardless of the style, the quality must be good.

An opening in the history of church music was the reinstatement of the cantor. Naturally in the early church this role was much more important, as the organist had not yet come into existence. Is the role discussed much today? What role should a cantor have besides the verses of the Responsorial Psalm? Is the role of the cantor a mere anachronism, dreamt up by liturgists, that does not really serve a liturgical need? Perhaps time will tell, but this dream should not be buried without a bit more thought and discussion.

Our aim—both for the choir as well as for the congregation—should not be to do more, but to do better compositions in a better way. The examination of conscience would go like this: Have I woefully abandoned the congregation to sing trite tunes and patched-up Broadway musicals out of fatigue and laziness? Have I abandoned some of the fine hymn tunes of the 16th century in favor of the sentimental texts and chromatic harmonies of the last century? (Charismatic renewal people should dwell especially long on this question.) Have I failed to seek out or compose new music that will inspire because I fear it will be difficult or I might not get a raise in pay? In other words: Am I in a rut?

The following observations deal with music, but with specific tendencies that are evolving in the American Church that are worthy of a second and sometimes critical look. Our liturgies lack a contemplative dimension. We are filling in all the silences; we are singing everything at the same speed and same dynamic level — slow and loud. Oh, for a bit of silence after the readings and after Communion! Most of the meditation texts that people insert at these points are distracting.

Has the alternating style really worked out between congregation and choir? Without repeating what was said about the contrast between the well-rehearsed choir and the struggling congregation, one must admit that few composers have successfully written for choir and congregation. For example, in the Bartolucci Masses based on Mass 8, the congregational part is often so short that it is not worth opening your mouth for. The exceptions, however, prove that it can be done. The Renaissance composers did not hesitate to build their Masses on well-known melodies. Perhaps this is the only way of helping the people participate and well. We have not exhausted this style, and more should be done with it in the future.

The question of acclamations is one of the new ones since the changes in the liturgy and one of the most challenging. The dialogue acclamations before the Preface do not seem to be getting off the ground; perhaps this has been caused by the changes in the melodies, so that one is never sure which melody to use. But the acclamations after the Words of Institution and the Great Amen have indeed led to an extended repertoire. Unfortunately, the acclamation after the Words of Institution is often too long and becomes not an acclamation but a lengthy composition that interrupts the flow of the canon. The Great Amen, on the other hand, does not have such a limitation and can give full rein to musical instincts. Although similar acclamations are in place after the reading of the Gospel, unfortunately we seem to have neglected them at that point. (Indeed, we have in general neglected the possibilities of creating the introduction needed—the buildup, that is—before the Gospel. A procession with the Gospel book and Easter candle and incense to the singing of a great Alleluia and its sequence made it clear to all that the reading of the Gospel was truly an important moment. We still have much to learn from that tradition.)

In the area of acclamations it seems that two liturgical moments have yet to be explored. The first of these is the end of Mass, the final *Deo Gratias* or Thanks Be to God. It would be helpful to have a repertoire of joyful, rousing acclamations for the end of Mass. This would be so much better than the usual hymn on so many occasions. Secondly, there is still some thought to be given to a Eucharistic Prayer of canon with acclamations. One of the canons for children's Masses has developed this ancient tradition, but it has not been worked out for any other canon. The present four canons are not written with this in mind, and attempts in this direction, especially in bringing back the *Sanctus* at various moments in the canon, have been forced and artificial. Perhaps Rome would look favorably on such a canon if it were presented as a way of enlarging our musical participation.

An acclamation that presents special problems is the end of the prayer following the Our Father: "For thine is the kingdom, ..." This text lends itself so well to singing, but seems badly placed psychologically between the two prayers that do not lend themselves as well to singing.

Several developments in the United States are questionable, not because they touch what is best or worst musically, but because they touch what is best or worst liturgically. First, if a rendition of the Our Father is sung by the choir alone, it is embarrassing for the celebrant to stand there with outstretched arms and be unable to sing along. Surely the people feel the same way.

A second development is the long Holy, Holy. We had tried so hard to clean up the liturgy and give it a certain simplicity, but now we may find a long concert between Preface and Anaphora rather than see a unity there.

Thirdly, the Preparation of the Gifts is sometimes blown up too much. Why there has to be an offertory hymn I'll never know. There are no traditional texts of offertory hymns, and the repertoire is meager. If there is a real offertory procession, something could be done; but even there we exaggerate by bringing up everything we can find around, so that the area around the altar gets cluttered.

Fourthly, we haven't found the solution yet to the place for the *Kiss of Peace* at Mass. It certainly disrupts the flow of the Mass where it is located now. In some churches, singing takes place too, but it conflicts with the *Lamb of God*. Here is a problem to be studied again by the Bishops Committee on the Liturgy. The Kiss of Peace where it is presently located is either disruptive or formalistic. Is it a moment for music? I wonder.

The second major question concerns the kind of person the church musician should be. First of all, he or she must be a professional in two categories — in music and in liturgy. The church is not the chosen realm of amateurs when it comes to music. It requires competency in both music and liturgy. (Sometimes one has to be a professional psychologist as well — but that would be another article.)

Sometimes one wonders if we haven't passed from the epoch of the left-footed organist to that of the I-IV-V guitarist. (If you are still among those organists whose right foot freezes to the swell box, or if you are one of those guitarists limited to two keys and three chords in each, branch out and practice.) There was much amateurism in church performance before the Council, and, unfortunately, the decrees on liturgy and music did not suddenly transform people. Perhaps, though, it made our musical limitations more evident. If we are now aware of this, then something important has been accomplished.

Our desire, however, to be professional in our standards and tastes does not come from elitism or snobbism, but because only then can we serve properly. This is what all the Church documents demand of us. Busy people have difficulty finding the time to practice, study, and do new things. Nevertheless, everyone should resolve that each year will find him or her an improved musician. Don't be afraid to seek professional help and criticism. People today are also more demanding: whether the style be the so-called folk idiom or Bach, it must be well done.

Not only must we consider it our task to improve our professional skills, but we must also consider it our mission to raise and develop the musical taste of our congregations. We underestimate our American Catholics. Tickets to concerts of fine music are hard to get; the performances of our major orchestras, recitals of our best singers, chamber music series—these are always sold out. People want the best, and so there is no need to stoop to the least common denominator. Many suspect that the priests are the troublemakers; it is they who demand the cheap stuff. But here we are running around in a vicious circle. We cannot give in here, but slowly create a new climate.

If slow progress has been made, it is because the strongest advocates of taste have often shown the most narrow understanding of the liturgical changes. Good taste then became too much the realm of the preservers of the classic tradition and not enough the challenge of the present and future. Those involved in the charismatic renewal should concern themselves about taste. The more emotional our participation is in worship, the higher our tastes must be. Only then can the proper balance be kept.

Next, the musician must be a professional with regard to liturgy. A professional knowledge of liturgy is so needed today. In addition to studies there must be a natural sensitivity to the needs of a worshiping body. Not all baptized people are qualified to be on the parish's liturgical committee. And not all creative people are qualified liturgists, either. Liturgy is not an arena for all creative people to show off their art. It requires a sensitivity to its own laws and inner dynamic. Liturgy is a science and art of its own. Creativity is needed, but within the parameters that the liturgical moment itself determines.

In addition to being a professional in music and liturgy, the church musician—if he or she is to have any credibility today—must be a person of prayer. The effectiveness of the church musician today will depend on his or her personal sensitivity to prayer. Perhaps this strikes you as strange and really unimportant. I would say just the contrary. If there is a gap between the liturgical musician in the Church today and the priests and faithful, it is precisely because musicians do not seem to be praying people. Perhaps, years ago, the personal witness was not as important because the whole of Catholic culture was supported by external social structures that took care of themselves. This is not true today. In a time of change the musician must be existentially and personally involved as the church works out new liturgical practices. They will not be worked out at committee tables, but by praying people.

We often forget to reflect on the profound, if not childlike, faith of a Mozart or Beethoven. Could Bach have devised such artistic but coherent solutions for chorus and faithful as shown in the Passions if he had not understood what prayer is about? To be a slick or even good craftsman is not enough. To be even extremely creative and gifted is not enough. The church musician must be a person of prayer.

There are a number of obstacles the musician has to face in the Church today. Some of these have been alluded to — especially the apparent lack of taste among some of our clergy. Such a problem is real. It can be overcome only when the credibility of the musician is looked at too. Only then will the confidence of the priest in the church musician be increased and will the musician be able to help and assist the priest. If the priest becomes convinced that you, too, are concerned about helping a congregation pray more profoundly, he is more inclined to listen. Perhaps we have to begin at that purely human level. Musicians who feel the image they must sustain is one of tantrums and displays of temper will never help convince anyone. Naturally we musicians get upset when the organ needs tuning or there is a cipher, but reasonableness will usually prevail with a bit of common sense. Musicians can be very humorless people, too.

But perhaps the greatest obstacle of all is our own frustration. We want to do the best, but we come away from every workshop and convention inspired and all enthused, only to find that nothing has changed back home. No one else seems to share our enthusiasm, and the salary remains the same. Perhaps what we all need are long-term goals. If we can see only to the next day, we become discouraged. If we look beyond and plan for a better future, we will have some ideals to keep us going. We have done amazingly well in these last fifteen years; and if all continues in this fashion, the '80s will be just as exciting. When I see how easily and spontaneously our children sing today and with what clarity they are able to read in church, what poise they possess, I feel we are on the right track.

God does not demand perfection of us overnight and understands our imperfect musical prayers. The mere fact that so many can come together at conventions to share experiences and give mutual support to one another is the most positive sign that all will move forward. Conventions should give one a sense of Church, of a larger struggling body, to counteract those more concrete and personal frustrations that come with the parish liturgy.

Something *has* happened in liturgical music since Vatican II, and it is just the beginning. If you continue to dedicate your talents to help God's people pray in music, then the glorious period will be in the not-too-distant future. To prepare that future you must all strive to develop your musical talents, your liturgical knowledge and sensitivity, and, above all, to deepen your own personal prayer-life.

THE DILEMMA OF PASTORAL MUSIC

Rev. John Melloh, SM
Director, Notre Dame Center for Pastoral Liturgy.

The Dilemma of Church

As a child I thought of the Church as a building; my family would go to church — meaning the building — to pray. During my grade school years, I thought of Church not only in terms of a building, but also in terms of the hierarchy — an ecclesiastical corporation, with the pope as president, bishops as vice-presidents and priests as corpoarate executives. In my unnuanced model, I didn't even think of myself, or the rest of the faithful, as stockholders. High school saw the introduction of the term "mystical body," with a stress on the social dimension of the Church, with Christ Jesus as Head. At that time I imaged the faithful, myself included, as tiny cells, quite insignificant, despite the protestations to the contrary of my religion teachers.

What is our dominant image of Church today? To think of the Church as people, a group, is not new. In fact, the first-generation Christians referred to themselves as *ecclesia*, which means the assembly, or the gathering. Christians identified themselves as the group or the coming together.

Another term used by these early Christians was *koinonia*, or fellowship. But it was not fellowship in the sense of Grover Whelan's bestowing the keys to the city or the image of "hail fellow well met." It indicated a sense of belonging; Christians belonging to one another — they had a stake in each other's living.

This was "Church" — a coming together in the name of Jesus. This Jesus willed to create a community through his death and resurrection that would be a sign to the world, a community that would judge and convict the world, whose judgment and conviction would be seen not in power tactics, but in lifestyle.

The mission of Jesus, as described by John, was "to gather the scattered children of God into unity" (11:52). Born into a world like ours — unfriendly, even hostile, strife-ridden and disunited — Jesus wished to call together into unity, into harmony, into concert all God's children. Disciples of Jesus would prove that life could be lived not in suspicion, hostility, fear and violence, but rather in peace, concert, love and mutual service. They were to do this by their sharing of faith, of vibrant belief in Jesus, which would move them to live as he did, by being a servant to all. The principle for living together was not rivalry and mutual exploitation, not competition and self-aggrandisement, but simply service in love.

The words of Jesus, "to serve," in Latin became *ministrare*, the root of our English words "minister" and "ministry." We are, as Church, as a People, called to minister to one another. And it is only within this wider context of Church that any specific ministries make sense.

Thus, the New Testament Churches saw this as their mission: to acknowledge the works of God and to be living evidence of God's salvific power through service, through ministry to one another. They would then stand as a sign of hope to the world.

The Dilemma of Ministry

Ministry today, as in the early Church, is primarily something that happens continuously. It is a quality of living more than it is a job. there is ministry in the caring for a newborn child, when a parent helps a child with homework, when a mother serves as reconciliation minister stopping siblings' squabblings, when an individual helps a neighbor in difficulty, when one visits someone who is sick, or gives directions to a stranger in the city, or car-pools to save a gallon, as Mr. Amoco suggests, and so on. The attitude that informs these actions makes them genuinely ministerial — service in love, not exploitation or for selfish interests.

Placing goods and talents at the service of the community is Christian ministry. It is not, we should note, liturgical ministry that is clearly evident in the New Testament Churches, but rather the ministries of reconciliation, healing, preaching; ministries of care and support. But liturgical ministries do derive from this wider context of ministerial activity — we are Church together because we have first been served by God in Christ Jesus; the example has been given to us that we might do likewise.

While the synoptic writers speak of the Eucharist in terms of the words over the bread and cup, John speaks of its meaning in terms of service — the washing of feet. Jesus celebrates the meaning of his life and death in the meal that we might discover the meaning of our lives in service to one another.

It is necessary to give this broader context to ministry, lest we reduce specific liturgical ministries to questions of mere correct performance. Liturgical ministry presupposes an attitude toward life; unless this attitude of service is understood, the roles in celebrtion become only a means of assuring the smooth running of the celebration. Readers, musicians, servers, welcomers — all may become preoccupied with the technicalities of their service and forget the meaning of the action.

Restoration of liturgical ministries, which had atrophied, is an inevitable consequence of our return to more ancient, New Testament models of Church. Within the liturgical context, the restoration of ministries is itself a symbol of the lifestyle that we as Christians are called to follow. Liturgical ministries are nothing more and nothing less than self-conscious ritualization of the shape of our lives — they speak without words about how our lives are spent in service to our God and to one another. Human beings become the means whereby our God reaches out to save us.

This is the dilemma of ministry: how are our ministries within the liturgical celebration intimately connected to our daily lives? How are our liturgical ministers in truth signs of transformation for us at worship? How does our ministry transform us as minister, transform those to whom we minister and ultimately transform our world?

The Dilemma of Leadership

New rites and new languages can be adopted in this post-Vatican II period without necessarily engaging those who use them in the real meaning and spirit of the new expressions. Liturgical reforms can be mere adjustments, perceived as new, within a closed structure of prescriptive norms.

It is the function of leadership to facilitate the free and meaningful integration of newer and, it is hoped, more vital expression of our life together as Church. Psychiatrist Thomas Szasz writes that there are two kinds of leadership: for dependence and for independence. A background for understanding such a statement may be taken from the Swiss psychologist Jean Piaget. He speaks of two categories of relationship: "authority relations" and "mutual relations." The first obtains in the situation in which one person interacts with another in a role of subservience; the one is the expert and the other is the follower. In this situation, the interaction strengthens superiority and reinforces subservience.

The second, mutual relations, obtains when parties act together as peers, or if not altogether peers, within a realm that allows each to contribute insights, knowledge, investments and commitments that are comparable. In this interaction, both learn the capacities and limitations of personal resources and understand their common interest.

If we speak of the dominant image of Church today as that of the Pilgrim Throng, and the image of ministry as that of service to one another in love, then it follows that the style of leadership that is called for is leadership based on mutuality rather than subservience. It is a leadership that calls forth responsibility—the ability to respond.

Leadership within the Church has less to do with the smooth running of projects, meetings and worship services than with the shaping and nurturing of a community. While, admittedly, leadership for dependence may produce achievements with fewer loose ends and may more facilely achieve its desired end product, it seems to pay less attention to the comonly held Christian belief that God's animating spirit is poured out on all the baptized and that each has a call to ministry.

Leadership for responsibility deals honestly with each individual in our Church as spirit-gifted, and it revolves around the quality of responding and being personally responsible. It is a leadership that enables rather than constricts; that calls forth rather than demands; that reverences rather than takes for granted. Leadership for responsibility and not dependence may not be the operating model in our dioceses, parishes, religious communities or families. If we would buy into such a model, then changes must be effected through a mutual effort.

Implied in the thought of the pastor who believes that to teach, rule and sanctify is a unilateral process belonging to him is that there are others who are to be taught, ruled and sanctified—without mutual cooperation. The pastoral music director who thinks that s/he is to decide by him/herself what will be sung, when, by whom and how sets him/herself up as musical demagogue. The parent who makes all decisions for the adolescent, without ever listening, is bound to reap the harvest that is sown. "Do not lord it over one another as the heathens do," advised (or commanded?) Jesus. And we are, each one of us, under this judgment.

Competencies must be respected. Piaget does not mean to suggest that in leadership roles we do not respect competencies, but rather wishes to suggest that we listen to one another, so as to understand and act in concert with one another—for the good of the entire assembly, for the community, for the fellowship.

Ignatius of Antioch, writing to the Ephesians, puts it this way: "Yes, one and all, you should form yourselves into a choir; so that in perfect harmony, and taking your pitch from God, you may sing in true unison and with one voice, as strings of a harp, to the Father through Jesus Christ." While he was speaking of communal worship, his advice applies to styles of leadership: take your pitch from God (not from IBM) and act in concert with one another (not out of rivalry or selfish interest) for the good of all (not just your own).

The Dilemma of Relationship

Fifteen years ago, Erik Routley wrote: "I would urge that for proper communication of the creative word of God in worship a much closer cooperation between minister, choirmaster, organist, choir, church management, education authorities and office-bearers is required than we normally look for. Too often—perhaps almost universally— each major participant in worship plays a solo without reference to anybody else" (p. 109).

Cooperation is requisite, not only for smooth running, not only for effective management, but because the very act of communication of the creative Word of God and the making, the positing of the sacramental acts requires it. Sacramental activity is not a solo performance;

it is an ecclesial action that demands cooperation before, during, and after, else we put the lie to it.

Routley continued: "Tensions between ministers and organists are lamentably frequent; where they are not openly apparent they often exist in the form of resigned resentments. The only way that occurs to some ministers or musicians of relating those tensions is simply take the line that cooperation is unnecessary anyway. Then the whole 'production' falls flat and people wonder why this has happened. Alternatively, one of the participants 'steals the show' or 'hogs the scene,' and because it is all in a religious context perhaps the unfortunate loser in this unlovely context will say that this is the Lord's will and keep quiet about it. All of which is very much to the detriment of public worship, or, at all events, it means that opportunities are being lost" (p. 109).

If the pastor sins by determining the hymn tunes, the settings for the acclamations, and so on, so too does the musician who makes these same judgments in isolation. Routley is strong in stating: "The minister of music who lets his minister of the gospel down by having no views and no representative part to play ought to mend his ways or leave his appointment" (p. 111). The same could be said of the pastor: the minister of the gospel who lets his minister of music down by having no views and no representative part to play ought to mend his ways or leave his appointment!

Teamwork — this is what is required. The teamwork between music and theology can be begun wherever there is Church: an assembly, a musician, a pastor, ministers. It will probably begin, Routley suggests, with repentance on the part of any who "hoped that their office would protect them from the demands of teamwork, and go on to a sense of discovery and fellowship," that is, move to the notion — in the concrete — of what it means to be *ecclesia, koinonia*.

Teamwork and dialogue are different from declaring one's turf and allowing no intruders. Just as that style of "academic freedom" that means I teach my discipline and you teach yours — is but a caricature of the real thing, so too can there be a caricature of parochial teamwork — I make my decision in my area and you make yours, and we keep our noses out of the decision-making process. Admittedly, such an approach is easier — Exxon does it all the time. Surely, Excedrin is not needed quite so often—plain aspirin will do. But—and be sure of this—I belong to you and you to me—has been replaced by an ersatz gospel, alien to the spirit of Christ Jesus.

The Dilemma of Volunteerism

To volunteer has nothing to do with money; it has everything to do with freedom and will. What the New Testament can show is that, in the main, the various ministries for specific Church leadership were not volunteer ministries. Individuals were called, chosen and then confirmed in that ministry, if they, after having been called, volunteered, that is offered themselves freely. A talent, gift was recognized, and then the individual was called to put it to specific use for the community. The community then confirmed the individual in that ministry.

And *this* is the point for us. Too often we have sought volunteers for this or that and have not first discerned the gifts and talents. The case was different in a parish where a friend is pastor. He surveyed the scene for a while and then said to this individual: I notice that you have good voice and have had training in music; I think that you should consider being a leader of song for our parish.

But the responsibility for the calling need not rest squarely on the pastor's shoulders alone. We—as this *ecclesia*—should be willing to suggest: "I see that you have a good way when you're visiting people in the hospital. You really put them at ease. Have you considered becoming a minister of the Eucharist to bring Communion to the sick?" Or again: "You really have a way with words and speak well in public. Have you thought about being a reader for our parish?" Examples could be multiplied.

This whole issue gets quite sticky when money enters the discussion. Merely using money as a means of assuring control—quality or otherwise—strikes me as not sufficiently Gospel-rooted. Both the salaried and the non-salaried are under the judgment of the same Gospel and they must, both of them, be subject to the demands of word and worship.

Some parishes absolutely need one or more full-time musicians who obviously should be salaried members of the pastoral team. They should receive a living wage (thank you, Leo XIII!) commensurate with their professional credentials, both in the area of music as well as that of liturgical knowledge. Stipends and salary should not merely be computed for the time of the performance, because at least 90% of the work takes place before the performance; while it may not be specifically noticed during the time of performance, it would be noticed in its absence.

This same parish may also require the services of other trained musicians—instrumentalists, song leaders, choir members. Some of these, too, may receive stipends; others may not. But all of this needs to be decided in honest and open dialogue before the fact. Asking for the services of an amateur (that is, one who is trained, even professionally, but does not "participate for gain or livelihood" and is thus not a professional in that sense) may be needed. Those matters of allocation of stipends need to be the concern of the parish council members who administer the budget. Saying to some individuals: "We just haven't the funds; we're really strapped financially, but we ask for your competencies" is quite a different thing from *expecting* (worse still, demanding) the surrender of one's gifts with no dialogue, no discussion concerning honorarium. (Do you see the leadership models at work here?)

Some points need further clarification:

1. Both the salaried and non-salaried have the same basic demands placed on them. Both need to be competent in what they are doing musically. The individual whose organ playing convinces the assembly that s/he is wearing galoshes and mittens should neither be salaried nor unsalaried; that individual is a menace to worship. The person who requires several baskets to carry a tune just cannot be a cantor. Those are the facts. So salaried and non-salaried individuals need musical competency.

Secondly those musically competent individuals need to become liturgically competent because they are subject, as is the rest of the body of believers, to the demands of the liturgical act. In an altercation with the organist, a friend of mine disputed the liturgical appropriateness of some of the selections chosen for the celebration. The reply was, "Well, I'm only a volunteer. What do you expect?" The answer, hard to hear, is that more is expected. Making musical judgments is insufficient—those judgments are to be scrutinized in light of the tradition of the communal worship. If a musician chooses funereal-sounding songs for the veneration of the cross on Good Friday, that individual sets him/herself up against the tradition of the Roman Church of the meaning of that act. A musician who has no understanding of the clearly stated purpose of the introductory rites of the Mass is liable to create a musical imbalance between the Liturgy of the Word and what is clearly preparatory. Let these examples suffice to demonstrate the principle.

2. Being a liturgical musician (or a liturgical artist in any field) means to surrender. It means to surrender the gift of music, the gift of architecture, the gift of dance, and so forth, to the community at prayer. And this means to narrow, or better, perhaps, to channel those talents. It means, for example, that the composer is not free to compose a setting for the Holy that dismisses congregational participation. It means that architects are liturgically irresponsible when they create a worship space that says in wood and stone that Church is hierarchy and congregation is a group of separated spectators. It means that cantors are not free to view their singing as a solo performance. It means that artists are not free to create a table for the Eucharistic meal that has none of the characteristics of a table or to have the table-altar dominate the other focus, the table of the Word. It means that presiders, who exercise the artistic ministry of leading folks in prayers, are not free to ignore the genuine role of other ministers.

We are all subject to the same Word and the same worship. We are not free to use our gifts, talents, competencies in the liturgical arena without having them subject to the basic demands of communal worship. Those talents we offer are not for private use, but are for a genuinely communal act; they are for the building up of the one Body of Christ. This is the dilemma of volunteer ministry. Questions of "volunteer" or "call," salary or no salary, private use or communal use need to be carefully scrutinized in dialogue.

To conclude, a convention is a time of festival. It is a time when we withdraw from the ordinary and experience the extraordinary — perhaps more exactly, experience the ordinary in an extraordinary way. We are tuned in. As Pieper put it, we are in tune with the world. Time — that chronic succession of moments — seems to elude us in the festival atmosphere. We celebrate, gathered together to tell our common story, to share experiences, to be with friends, to meet new friends, to be of "one mind and one heart." Coming together in the name of Jesus, we discuss and dispute our common concerns in his service. As believers we gather in convention, not only to learn from one another, but to be with one another as a group of pray-ers. We join together to offer our daily prayer and to share the supper of the Lord's table — ordinary, yet extraordinary.

Nonetheless, as we have come together, we too shall be dismissed — the second necessary part of convocation. And so the question remains: To what are we called? What is needed?

1. We need ever ourselves to become living witnesses of what it means to be Church. Our ministry is a ministry of being a "sacrament," sign — and that is a full-time occupation, both in worship and outside worship.

2. We need to look closely at our existential model of Church to examine how we behave as Church. We need to grow to be a people who wash one another's feet.

3. We need to create continually ministry that expresses and calls forth new life together.

4. We need to help build styles of leadership that coax responsibility — the ability to respond — from each of God's spirit-anointed.

5. We need to recognize each other's gifts, which are surrendered for our common life, and we need to create parish teams that thrive on relationships based on mutuality.

6. We need honesty in our budget and structures for improvement.

7. We need, in a word, to be perfect as our heavenly Father is perfect.

I leave you with the words of Erik Routley: "Perhaps the future of the church's communication with the world lies with the prophecy and priesthood of the musicians who handle mysteries and make them friendly, who can speak the unspeakable in a language that uses no words, in whose art action and thought are joined, in whose hands applied science is the servant of beauty and honor. In every place where the gospel is being preached, this secret is waiting for its revelation" (p. 120).

REFERENCES: Philibert, Paul, "Leadership for Responsibility" *Liturgy* 24 (1979).
Routley, Eric, *Music Leadership in the Church*, Abingdon Press, 1967, Nashville, Tenn.
Searle, Mark, *Ministry and Celebration*, Office of Worship, La Crosse, Wisc.

THE MUSICIAN AS MINISTER

Rev. Nathan Mitchell, OSB
Faculty, Archabbey of St. Meinrad, Ind.

In the year 1747, at the age of 63, Johann Sebastian Bach made a journey to the court of King Frederick of Prussia at Potsdam. Actually, old Bach didn't care a fig about the king; he had gone to Potsdam to visit one of his many talented sons, Carl Philip Emmanuel, who had become Kapellmeister at Frederick's court. It seems, however, that when the Bach-mobile roared into town, some of Frederick's musical cronies caught wind of it — and before old Bach could even change out of his traveling costume, he was whisked off, periwig and all, to the palace. Frederick wanted the old man to improvise a few trifles on his new Silbermann piano. (Frederick, incidentally, was one of those rare musical monarchs who enjoyed being in the *avant garde* of Europe's cultural life; he correctly predicted that the pianoforte would become the hottest item since sackbutts and rebecs.) In any case Bach obliged the king by improvising fugues in four, five and six parts. And just to show everybody who was really the boss, Bach then asked Frederick to give him a fugue subject of the king's own making on which to improvise. The king promptly tossed off a complicated, chromatic little tune in C minor — and Bach astonished everyone present by improvising a perfect fugue right on the spot.

After Bach got back home to Leipzig, he wrote an extremely oily and ingratiating letter to Frederick (after all, Bach's boy worked for the king), and enclosed a set of compositions — chiefly canons and ricercare — based on the tune Frederick himself had composed. Bach called the set *Das Musikalische Opfer*, "The Musical Offering." The canons and fugues of "The Musical Offering" are an ingenious *tour de force* of 18th-century contrapuntal technique. Bach does everything imaginable with Frederick's chromatic tune: he slows it down, he speeds it up, he turns it upside down, he runs it backward, he chases it around the circle of fifths. But there is one canon in "The Musical Offering" that is particularly spectacular. Bach called it *"Canon a due per tonos"* (canon in two voices through [all] the keys) — and he wrote a clever little Latin phrase at the top of the canon: *"Ascendenteque modulatione ascendat Gloria Regis"* (as the modulation ascends, so may the Glory of the King ascend). Bach was a sly old fox — and this little canon shows just how sly he could be. The canon begins in the key of C minor, but by the time you get to the end of the first canonic imitation, you discover that somehow, some way, Bach has managed to modulate up to the key of *D minor*. The same thing happens again: you're running along pleasantly in the key of D minor when all of a sudden you get to the end of the second canonic imitation and discover that you're now in the key of *E minor!* And for the life of you, you can't figure out how you got there. And that's not all: Bach keeps the canonic structure absolutely, perfectly intact. It is a perfect canon at the fifth, which somehow manages to modulate through all the keys — C minor, D minor, E minor, F minor, etc. — until the piece ends right back in the key of C minor, where it all started.

What Johann Sebastian Bach had given the king was an endlessly rising canon that could, theoretically, go on forever — stretch all the way to musical infinity. And paradoxically, through a series of strange musical loops, Bach manages to destroy our sense of beginnings and endings: the music begins where it ends and ends where it begins. Like the symbolic circle that seems to have neither beginning nor ending, Bach has given us, in his endlessly rising canon, a musical image of infinity, a musical paradox of infinite possibilities.

The story of Bach's trip to Potsdam — and the music that resulted from his journey — reveals something profound about the relation between musical art and the human hunger for infinity, for transcendence, for what Christians would call "the vision of God." It tells us, among other things, that the human search for God is an endlessly rising canon that begins where it ends — and ends where it begins. This probably sounds paradoxical—and it should. The human journey toward God—and God's journey toward us—*is* a paradox, an intricate fugue that brings us, at the end, back to the beginning. Perhaps the poet T.S. Eliot said it best in the last of his *Four Quartets*.

> What we call the beginning is often the end
> And to make an end is to make a beginning.
> The end is where we start from...
> Every phrase and every sentence is an end and a beginning,
> Every poem an epitaph. And any action
> Is a step to the block, to the fire, down the sea's throat
> Or to an illegible stone: and that is where we start.
> We die with the dying:
> See, they depart, and we go with them.
> We are born with the dead:
> See, they return, and bring us with them...
> We shall not cease from exploration
> And the end of all our exploring
> Will be to arrive where we started
> And know the place for the first time.
>
> —"Little Gidding," Section V

Both Eliot and Bach are telling us—one through the medium of language, the other through the medium of music—that the human hunger for God is as infinite, and as intricate, as art. Artists are, in fact, the people who confront us most uncompromisingly with the "paradox of infinity." And for this reason, artists are perhaps our surest guides on the journey toward God.

The specific topic at hand is the ministry of one special group of artists in the Christian community: the musicians—those much-maligned, much-misunderstood merry-makers who help us hear what God sounds like. First, the musician's ministry in the Church can be summarized in a single word: *mystagogue*. A mystagogue is not an insect, nor is it the name of a fatal disease, nor is it an aphrodisiac like amyl nitrite. A mystagogue is simply a human being who initiates other human beings into mystery—a person who guides us in our search for beauty ever ancient and ever new. Every musician is a mystagogue who uses the symbols of sound to reveal something new and beautiful about the holy God who hears. As mystagogue, the musician confronts us with the paradox of infinity; stretches our imagination about God; and leads us through the strange labyrinthine loops of an endlessly rising canon that carries us deeper and deeper into mystery. If it is still unclear what a mystagogue is, think of Bach: he was and remains the musical mystagogue *par excellence.*

Like all ministers, musicians help us discover new ways to explore old mysteries. But this is not as easy a task as it may appear. For centuries, traditional Catholic theology has assumed that the surest path to God is the one that leads through the discursive reasoning power of human intellect. God is, above all, a *mind* — a supremely gifted intelligence, overwhelming in its breadth and depth, razor-sharp in its power to discern true from false, virtue from vice. In short, we have been conditioned to believe that God is a cosmic intellect, and that human intellects (however feeble and fallible they may be) are the best examples of God's image in us. This has been, in fact, the fundamental tenor of Western theology ever since Augustine appealed to the operations of human will and intellect as a source for understanding God's own trinitarian life.

Where does this leave the artist? At the bottom of the pile, usually. The Church has often regarded artists as people whose minds and morals are too weak to serve as secure models for theology or Christian life. It's as though being an artist were slightly indecent, immoral — or at any rate, imperfect. Perhaps it is for this that we have hundreds of canonized theologians, but we still don't recognize St. Ludwig van Beethoven, St. Franz Schubert, St. Pierluigi da Palestrina, or St. Antonio Vivaldi. After nearly two millenia, the Church is still reluctant to accept the ministry and theology of the musician.

It is necessary to explore some of the unique gifts the ministry of musician brings to the Christian assembly. Clearly, there is a distinctive spirituality for artistic persons in the Church — and it is this spirituality that shapes our pastoral ministry for and among people. So the first thing is to outline a "spirituality for Christian artists." This will lead to some conclusions about the mystagogic ministry of the musician.

A Spirituality for Artists

Artists are easy to admire — and also very easy to dislike. Artists are, after all, the militant revolutionaries, the guerrilla warriors of the human psyche; and a Church that admires discipline and uniformity finds it difficult to accommodate them. Besides, artists have a disconcerting tendency to play by their own rules: they ambush us with unaccustomed ways of seeing, hearing and feeling; they pry deep into our sensibilities; they smoke us out of the caves and force us to look straight at the light. We don't like that. We don't like people who are both supremely gifted and supremely mad. But that's what art is: a passionate, seductive madness that grips us the way blackjack grips a gambler. We leave the artistic experience feeling simultaneously guilty and purified, like thieves who have stolen fire from the gods. Is it any wonder that Plato thought poets and musicians were too much for the Republic to handle?

Outlined below are some elements of a spirituality that embrace both the madness and the giftedness of artistic people in the Church. Such a spirituality is neither easy to identify nor simple to describe. For one thing, what often passes for Christian spirituality is little more than cultural garbage liberally sanitized by quotations from the Bible. If this remark seems ungenerous, chalk it up to my experience as a seminary professor. It isn't everywhere that you can hear Gail Sheehy's mandatory mid-life crisis and John's account of Jesus' passion talked about as though they were consubstantial and co-eternal. Nor is it everywhere that you can hear self-help, self-growth and self-awareness spoken of with the hushed reverence once reserved for theological discussions of the Trinity. But let that pass. As I understand it, art is not the same thing as therapy — nor is spirituality the same thing as transcendental self-attention. An artist is neither an emotional cripple who needs help, nor a degenerate sinner who needs absolution. An artist is simply a crazy, gifted person who is godlike because God too is crazy and gifted: crazy enough to fall in love with human beings — and gifted enough to transform this messy relationship into a perfect work of art called Jesus Christ.

To speak about a spirituality for artists and designers is thus to speak about a Christian way of life for people who are crazy, gifted and godlike. It is to speak of falling in love with the things of earth — with color, shape, sound, form, texture, water, dirt, stones, trees and (above all) people. It is to speak about the way a brook-pebbled surface interacts with sunlight on a late afternoon in the middle of April.

It is to speak about the geometry of prayer in a 12th-century Cistercian church so sensitive to sound that a pin dropped in its nave creates a full set of harmonic overtones. It is to speak about symbols so exquisite that they signal simply by being themselves — simply by being bread and salt, water and wine, oil and musk. It is to speak, paradoxically, about the visible colors of music and about the tangible warmth of burnished copper and natural oak. It is to speak, as the American composer John Cage does, of quartets for heartbeat, bulldozer, landslide and prepared piano.

The first element of a Christian spirituality for artists, then, is the process of falling in love — like God — with the "impure poetry" of this earth. The impure poetry of earth was the recurring theme of Pablo Neruda, the Chilean writer and political Marxist who was also Thomas Merton's favorite poet. At first blush, there is something intensely incongruous about this affection between Merton the Christian monk and Neruda the confessed Marxist. But if you think about it for a moment, the incongruity vanishes. Both Merton and Neruda were poets, artists who made raids on the unspeakable. And in every poet, in every artist, there dwells both atheist and ascetic, both libertine and monk, both Narcissus and Goldmund. Every artist (and this includes the musician) is simultaneously a hidden hermit and a political subversive, an anonymous ascetic and a howling philanderer.

This dual identity of the artist was eloquently described by Pablo Neruda some years before his death in a short essay entitled "Toward an Impure Poetry." Poets, Neruda insisted, are simply people who succumb to the curious attractiveness of the earth, people who see clearly the "confused impurity of the human condition," people who celebrate "the abiding prescence of the human." One cannot be an artist, Neruda declares, without loving the impure poetry of earth: the meat and eggs and seeds that create our glory and our messiness. The abiding presence, the confused impurity of the human condition: love for this is what makes the artist crazy and gifted and godlike.

An artist is free, like God, to embrace the whole creation: its sweat and smoke, its lilies and urine, its perfection and impurity. But artists also know that imagination's liberty is purchased at the price of an exacting discipline. Art is, in fact, the supreme asceticism — and every artist's vocation includes a pilgrimage to the desert, a season of solitude, an eremetical toughness that shrinks the stomach and sharpens the vision. For the artist, Lent is a perpetual season; it is the inhabited universe of creative people.

There is an old Jewish story that says that God created the world not by filling up dead space with objects and things — but by *withdrawing* from space so that life in all its incredible variety could emerge and reveal itself. To put it another way, God "fasted" from space, *drew back,* so that the earthly beauty of plants and animals could shine in a human, habitable world. God creates by *fasting;* God creates by making *self* small so that *other* can live.

What this story says about God's own chosen asceticism could also be said about human artists. Think, for example, of the sculptor who stands before a block of stone and asks *not* "What can I make with this," but rather "How can I let the form and beauty already present in this stone emerge and reveal itself?" Like God, the sculptor fasts: he or she is not interested in "filling up space" but in chiseling away the debris so that the life already present in stone can reveal itself.

Poets provide another example of this supremely ascetic discipline of art. We often think of poets as people who use lots of words — but in fact, just the opposite is true. The poet *fasts* from language, just as the sculptor fasts from stone and God from space. It is the poet's task to make a clearing in language, to cut down the undergrowth of careless, inattentive speech so that the deeper world of human experiences can reveal itself new, naked, fresh and different. Poets approach language not as self-conscious masters but as self-effacing ascetics. Listen for a moment to this short poem by Robert Frost and you will see what I mean:

> Nature's first green is gold,
> Her hardest hue to hold.
> Her early leaf's a flower;
> But only so an hour.
> Then leaf subsides to leaf.
> So Eden sank to grief,
> So dawn goes down to day.
> Nothing gold can stay.

The experience Frost describes in this poem is altogether ordinary; we've all seen and felt what the poet sees and feels: the first green growth of spring doesn't last; leaves fall and are replaced by others; dawn gives way to day—and Eden, that primordial symbol of human happiness and harmony, sinks down into grief and misery. Frost is telling us, of course, about impermanence and loss—about the loss in nature and about the more bitter human loss of innocence. But notice that Frost tells us these things not by piling up words and explanations (as I have just done)—but by fasting from language, by choosing only a few lean words, none of them more than two syllables long.

Every artist is, then, both hedonist and monk, voluptuous epicure and contemplative ascetic. Music is surely a supreme example of the artist's dual identity. We create music *not* by saturating an environment with sound—which would be Muzak, not music—but by *fasting from noise* so that new sounds, new arrangements of pitch and rhythm and color, can emerge and be heard for the first time, as though we were present at the creation. We create music as much by creating silence as by creating sound. It is this controlled alteration of sound and silence that distinguishes *music* from mere acoustic pollution. Bach's endlessly rising canon—the opening example—is a spectacular example of musical asceticism at its finest. Working with nothing more than eight measures of a fugue subject in the key of C minor, Bach creates a musical metaphor of infinity; he pushes our imaginations to the brink and puts us face-to-face with the infinite possibility of God.

The artist as host (hostess). The second element of a spirituality for artists is hospitality. Hospitality is the art of creating a habitable environment for human beings. It has been said that the ultimate purpose of art is to render the "highest justice to the visible universe" (Flannery O'Connor), to create a world that human beings can inhabit. Whatever the medium may be—the language of poets, the brick and glass of architects, the stone of sculptors, the sound and silence of musicians—art seeks to create living space, breathing space for human inhabitants. And art that serves the Christian community is no exception: it too creates environments for people, not monuments for God. God, the prophet Nathan told David, doesn't need a house—and wouldn't live in one even if David built it. God goes where the people go, because God too is a pilgrim, a wanderer.

But this pilgrim God is also a host (or hostess), one who creates

The Musician as Minister: MITCHELL

human space by setting a table for the hungry. And the proof of this is to be found at the beginning and end of the Bible. Has it ever struck you that the Bible begins and ends with food? The story of humanity's tumultuous relationship with God begins with food in the garden of Genesis and ends with the Supper of the Lamb in the Apocalypse. Eating got us into trouble in the first place—and eating will save us in the end (a wholesome thought that ought to bring mighty consolation to dieters!) In both Genesis and Apocalypse, God is a culinary artist, a host, a table companion. Where God is, there is food. And by the same token, humanity's "original sin" was nothing more or less than a refusal of God's hospitality: God threw a party and we decided to brown-bag it instead.

God's culinary artistry, God's hospitality, is an archetypal symbol of what every artist intends to do for human beings. Artists, too, feed and nurture the world. But there is more. A work of art is not only nourishment, it is also a symbol of the future—of that "happier order of things" when God and humans will again be table companions. Ultimately, art points to a reconciled universe, to a world healed and restored, to a human environment redeemed from ugliness. And this is true even when the artist's own life suffers painful diminishment, even when the artist is convinced that the "happier order" promised by God cannot be found in the world.

Nelly Sachs was a German Jewess who managed to escape to Sweden during Hitler's "final solution" of the "Jewish problem." Confronted with the unspeakable horror of the Holocaust, Mrs. Sachs found that she had nothing recognizably human left—except the power of language. Mrs. Sach's poetry is an anguished chronicle of human destruction, written for survivors who know that in a genocidal nightmare no one really survives. Her poetry does not raise the dead back to life—but it does raise a solitary human voice in a world no longer human or habitable. Here is Nelly Sach's poem entitled "O the Chimneys":

> O the chimneys
> On the ingeniously devised habitations of death
> When Israel's body drifted as smoke
> Through the air—
> Was welcomed by a star, a chimney sweep,

A star that turned black
Or was it a ray of sun?

O the chimneys!
Freedomway for Jeremiah and Job's dust —
Who devised you and laid stone upon stone
The road for refugees of smoke?
O the habitations of death
Invitingly appointed
For the host who used to be the guest —

O you fingers
Laying the threshold
Like a knife between life and death —

O you chimneys,
O you fingers,
And Israel's body as smoke through the air!

It isn't possible to comment on a poem like this one. We can only listen to it and hear a woman creating human space for unimaginable grief. And in that lies Nelly Sach's act of artistic hospitality: she gives us space to mourn; she opens the mouth of a wound that lets us hear human voices weeping in the nightmare.

My second example of artistic hospitality is a more familiar musical one. We all know the basic facts of Beethoven's biography: his unhappy childhood with an alcoholic father; his disappointing love-life; his miserable relationship with his brother and nephew; his descent into deafness. Beethoven's life is a Freudian nightmare, a textbook example of damaging psychological traumas. We know too that Beethoven's final symphonic creation — the monumental Ninth Symphony — was written when the composer was, for all practical purposes, stone deaf. And yet this final symphonic statement concludes with a triumphant "hymn to joy." Beethoven's final "assessment" of the world — a world that had brought him incredible grief and excruciating physical deformity — was a mind-boggling hymn of praise. As an artist, Beethoven reacted to a life that had brought him overwhelming misery by creating a habitable world of sound in which all of us can live. His ultimate symphonic testament was a supreme act of nurturing hospitality. Faced with his own death and deafness, Beethoven set a musical table at which all of us have feasted ever since. His hospitality was no accident; Beethoven knew what he was doing — and said so, in his Heiligenstadt Testament, written in 1802. Let me quote it, briefly:

> For me there can be no relaxation in human society .... I must be entirely alone, and except when the utmost necessity takes me to the threshold of society I must live like an outcast.... Sometimes I have been driven by my desire to seek the company of other human beings, but what humiliation when someone, standing beside me, heard a flute from afar off while I heard nothing.... Such experiences have brought me close to despair, and I came near to ending my own life — only my art held me back, as it seemed impossible to leave this world until I have produced everything I feel it has been granted me to achieve.... It has not been easy, and more difficult for an artist than for anyone else. Oh God, you look down on my inner soul, and know that it is filled with love of humanity and the desire to do good....

Through his music Beethoven became the consummate host, spreading a feast and creating a human environment where all of us can find happiness and strength. Despite his painful life — or perhaps *because* of it — Beethoven's music became a sacrament of that "more cheerful order of things," of a world renewed and reconciled.

Respect for symbols. These reflections on "artistic hospitality" lead to a third quality of spirituality for artists and designers: respect for symbols. Traditionally, Roman Catholics have thought of themselves as a community where symbolism enjoys supreme attention and reverence. As a matter of fact, however, Catholics are increasingly inept at identifying what symbols are and how they "work." Perhaps it's because in common English usage "the symbolic" is opposed to "the real" — as though contact with the one eliminates contact with the other. Perhaps, too, it's because symbols are often regarded as "objects," "pictures," or "things" that "represent something else" and thus have no independent life of their own.

First of all, then, let me say that symbols are neither objects nor things — nor are they primarily "representational." Symbols are *actions*, transactions; they are verbs, not nouns. In other words, symbols are generative; they create clash, tension and movement. In language, for example, metaphor leads toward symbol precisely because metaphor generates clash and tension by putting two things together that appear not to belong together. Encountering a good metaphor is like accidentally sitting on a porcupine: the event generates movement — and if it doesn't, there's something wrong with you or with the porcupine. Metaphor thus creates motion in language — and when that motion is regularly re-activated (in the context, say, of a single poem or of a poet's work), a "linguistic symbol" is what happens. The "moment in the rose garden," the "moment in and out of time" is, for instance, T.S. Eliot's generative symbol for the experience of transcendence in a world inescapably bound to history.

Christians have traditionally believed that the human encounter with God occurs within symbolic media — and that those media are active, fleshly, historical and even "wordly." This is why the central symbol of Christians is a human being: Jesus of Nazareth, whose flesh and history are to be taken seriously. Jesus is understood to "symbolize" the ultimate transaction between God and the world precisely *because* of his humanity — not in spite of it. This is why Christians have classically resisted any doctrine that denies or denigrates the true humanity of the Lord. In a word, Jesus reveals "God-ness" in our world precisely in and through the transactions of human flesh — and because of that, Jesus is the ultimate symbol — the "sacrament" of the meeting with God. Jesus *is* a symbol *simply by being himself* — simply by being a man who lives, works, eats, drinks, listens, heals, blesses, loves and dies.

And this is in fact true of all symbols: symbols "work" simply by being themselves. If one has to "make" the symbol "mean something," then what one has is a mistake, not a symbol. All Christian spirituality appeals to the ambiguous power of symbols, but the spirituality of artists and musicians relies on them to a preeminent degree. Perhaps this point is nowhere more fully evident than in architecture. Along with the culinary crafts of cooking and meal-making, architecture is an aboriginal art: it carries us closest to our human origins. Archaic humans not only sought food and made meals, they also sought shelter and made dwellings. And we've been doing it ever since. I suspect that the reason for this is to be found in the inherently symbolic character of the human body itself. Our bodies are perceived not merely as tools, objects or instruments but as dwellings, as habitations. As such, the body is the prime symbol of human interdependence, of the need for dwelling together, of the need to share habitation as food is shared in a meal. In a very profound sense, meals and dwellings make us human — and in fact they became the premiere evolutionary characteristics that distinguished us from our closest primate cousins, the baboons and the chimpanzees.

Architecture inevitably confronts us with the ancient symbols of the body, the body-personal and the body-corporate. Perhaps this is why architecture exerts such an enormous psychological impact on human inhabitants. Bodies and buildings are woven together in a dance as ancient as our origins. Christianity recognized this fact in its ancient rites for the consecration of a church. In effect, the building was treated as a body: it was washed, anointed, fed and clothed. These rites, as exotic as they are, were not mere Gallican distortions of Christian piety; they were in fact an acknowledgement of the ancient anthropological connection between human body and human building. They were also a frank psychological recognition that buildings have skins, organs, wombs, and faces. The image of the Church as mother is not only theological; it is also — and perhaps more profoundly — psychological.

The archaic symbolic connection between human bodies and human buildings is especially evident in the Cistercian architecture of the 12th century. The abbey church at Le Thoronet in southern France was built about 1135 A.D. and eloquently represents what St. Bernard liked to call "geometry at the service of prayer." Like most Cistercian churches, the one at Le Thoronet uses familiar architectural devices aimed at simplicity of style: a drastic reduction of visual stimuli and the use of perfect geometrical proportions. The result, of course, is a kind of contemplative elegance: quiet, straightforward, unadorned. The stones speak simply as stone — as stone interacting with stone, as stone interacting with light. And of course that sort of architectural statement was entirely congruent with the Cistercian ideology of contemplative peace and freedom from distracting stimuli.

But the curious thing about the church at Le Thoronet is its acoustics. Visually, the stimuli are drastically reduced: there are no paintings on the walls, no carvings on the capitals of pillars, no gargoyles on the choir stalls, no mosaics, and nothing but natural colors. But acoustically, if I may switch metaphors in mid-stream, the church at Le Thoronet is a horse of a different color. The building is so sensitive to sound that a pin dropped in the nave produces a full set of harmonic overtones and can be heard in the apse about thirty yards away. The geometric proportions of the church were such that the sound of singing voices in that space would give your body an "acoustical rub-down." The monks who sang the Divine Office in that building were actually being massaged by sound, their bodies were responding actively (though unconsciously) to constant subtle sonic stimuli. No wonder those monks liked to go to choir—they were being massaged by the sounds and spaces of the building itself.

At the church of Le Thoronet, visual austerity was more than adequately compensated by acoustic sensuality. Body and building melded into a single symbol of the human church at prayer. While the monks chanted, the building massaged them; single-minded austerity joined the impure poetry of earth to create a symbol of the church, earthly and unearthly. And like all good symbols, this one spoke for itself, and required neither explanation nor apology.

In the final analysis, perhaps it is just this combination of austerity and sensuality—of asceticism and impure poetry—that marks the spirituality of the Christian artist and musician. Like the crazy gifted God of Jesus Christ, such a person joins the familiar human with the unfamiliar "other," the ascetic with the hedonist, Narcissus with Goldmund. Like God, the Christian artist is a contemplative with dirt under the fingernails, someone who simultaneously casts shadows and gives off light. Perhaps the great modern architect Louis Kahn said it best when he wrote:

> Silence—the unmeasurable, desire to be, desire to express, the source of new need—meets Light—the measurable, giver of all presence, the measure of things already made—at a threshold which is inspiration, the sanctuary of art, the Treasury of Shadow. I said that all material in nature—the mountains and the streams and the air and we—are made of light which has been spent, and this crumpled mass called material casts a shadow, and the shadow belongs to the Light.

Shadows and light, asceticism and impure poetry, hospitality and respect for symbols: these are the elements of a spirituality for artistic people in the Church.

Implications for the ministry of musicians. The musician called to minister in the church is a *prophet,* not a caretaker. By this I mean that the musician challenges us with new ways to explore old mysteries. It is the musician's task to stretch the human imagination about God, to invite us to think about God with our bodies, our skins and our ears, and not merely with our intellects.

The musician exercises a ministry of artistic *hospitality* in the church. The musician's goal is to create a human, habitable world — an acoustic environment in which the mystery of God can be explored.

Musicians who serve the prayer and celebration of the Christian community do not have to assume another identity in order to be ministers. In other words, musicians are ministers *because* they are artists — not in spite of it. Musicians do not have to become "somebody else" in order to legitimate their ministry; their service *is* their art; their ministry *is* their music.

The minister of music is a mystagogue, someone who initiates others into mystery, someone who guides the community in its search for beauty ever ancient and ever new.

THE ANIMATOR

Rev. Joseph Gelineau, SJ

Rev. Gelineau, SJ is a virtuoso animator in Moret-sur-Loing, France. This article was translated from the French by Gina Doggett.

Ever since the time of the earliest Christian communities, their gatherings have been essential. It is on these occasions that Christians have always shared the Word of God, their goods, and the eucharistic bread. Like the Servant they celebrate, the Christ and Lord living in them through the Holy Spirit, Christians are all in service to one another. In order to maintain and perpetuate this mutual service, certain members of the community are invested with a ministry or spontaneously fill certain functions, such as the service of the Word, service to the poor, or the service of the table. These are not mere social duties that call for ordinary competence and dedication; they are ministries, or "charisms"—gifts of the Spirit for the building of the Church (I Cor. 14:26).

Church ministries have become both diverse and interdependent, as St. Paul envisioned them. Their makeup has evolved quite a bit over the course of history. Even if the organized, hierarchial triple ministry of the second century (episcopacy, presbytery, diaconate) had crystallized, the functions of these different orders would still have changed considerably by now. In any case, they are defined much less by the actual tasks involved as by their significance. In actuality, ministries develop and fade away, change, or reappear *according to the needs of the people.*

In the New Testament, ministries of the Word are predominant

The Animator: GELINEAU

(e.g., the work of the Apostles and itinerant evangelists, prophets and local preachers). Service ministries are also well represented. However, there is scarcely any reference to liturgical ministries. The present-day art of presiding over a celebration can hardly be linked to the gift of leadership that is mentioned in one of the many lists of charisms in I Corinthians! Indeed, it was not until the organization of congregations in the fourth century that liturgical ministries took on importance and definition. During the Middle Ages, liturgical functions were performed primarily by members of the clergy. Little by little, in the West at least, the priest assumed practically all of these roles. Only since Vatican II has a new division of responsibilities been emerging, with new or renewed ministries appearing in liturgy.

From Commentator to Animator

The role that we call *animateur* arose from a need to help the faithful participate in the liturgy. In the 20 years before the Second Vatican Council, when the liturgy was still entirely in Latin and controlled to the most minute detail, the push for "pastoral' renewal in the liturgy sought ways to enable the people to understand and participate. This was the origin in many countries, of the commentator. His role consisted of finding certain "holes" in the liturgy that were left open by the rubricists so that the words of a prayer, a song, or a rite could be inserted in the native language of the faithful. The commentator did the introductions, the invitations, and the admonitions, and made commentaries and paraphrases for the weekly celebration. Most commonly, this pastor/liturgist — almost always a priest — was also the one who encouraged the congregation to participate in singing. Nevertheless, the commentator and his duties were by no means considered "liturgical"; he was seen as a kind of parasite who was only tolerated because of his apparent usefulness.

The reform of Vatican II, with the attendant use of living languages, opened the way for a redivision of roles in the celebration according to the real needs of the people and their various abilities. This allowed for the appearance — or reappearance — of the reader, the psalmist, the cantor; and eventually, the welcome service, the collect, the intentions of common prayer, and so forth. The role of the commentator dissolved. It was superfluous to make "explanations" and "commentaries" during the celebration now that the words and signs had regained their direct meaning to the people. Any sort of dubbing, glossing, or reporting became irritating. Poetry, music, symbols—these things are not to be explained; they are to be experienced. And if introductions to the day's liturgy, or to a reading, or to an unfamiliar rite would still be useful, then it was up to the one presiding to make them, not an additional minister.

Still, at least in some parishes, it seems that the disappearance of the erstwhile commentator left a gaping hole. It is all well and good that everyone—celebrant, reader, choir member, acolyte, and so on—is "doing solely and totally what the nature of things and liturgical norms require of him," as urged by the Constitution on the Sacred Liturgy (#28). But with so many gears, don't we need someone to make them mesh and turn harmoniously?

A Central Nervous System

In biology we learn that the mark of a complex living organism is an extraordinarily developed central nervous system, which receives sensations, emits motor impulses, and coordinates movements. Something similar happens in a liturgical celebration. In a small gathering for which every function is adequately filled, a moderately gifted priest can manage to coordinate the celebration. However, for a larger group, or a heterogeneous group, or at complex functions—where the presider is often distant or lacks communicative presence—there is commonly a need for a *coordinator*.

This need is not new. For solemn or pontifical ceremonies, which have at times been quite complex, a liturgical "master of ceremonies" has been there to remind everyone, at all the right moments, what had to take place. But this person was concerned only with the rites and the ministers of the Church establishment, and not at all with the people and their prayer.

Going a little farther back in history, there was the deacon. The early deacon—unlike the deacon of our *missae solemnis* who simply assisted the priest—was primarily at the service of the congregation. He told them when to pray, when to stand, kneel, process, and so on; sometimes he took collection; he gave all the cues: for the dismissal of the catechumens, the beginning of the Eucharistic Prayer, when to

The Animator: GELINEAU

come forward for communion, for the final dismissal; in some cases, the deacon intoned the chants. In short, he was the constant link between the altar and the nave, between the ritual action and the participants. He personified the "central nervous system" of the celebration.

A revival of such a role is needed today, as much to help the gathering in its prayerful participation as to free the priest to do his service of presiding—if he indeed wants to give up roles other than his own! The coordinating role no longer requires an ordained deacon, either. It is a function that any competent member of the congregation can carry out.

The Animation of Singing

Recent developments in the role of the coordinator have underlined—at least in some countries—the importance of the animation of singing. This is easy to understand, because, especially since Vatican II, singing represents the main form of active congregational participation. In areas where singing participation does not happen to be traditional (as in the Germanic countries), it has been necessary to encourage the congregation to sing, to assure them; in a word, to *animate* them, so that they discover through their own experience the value of common sung prayer. But even in those countries where the faithful sing well and voluntarily, the usefulness of an animator as an individual minister is apparent. Likewise, in a smaller parish, although the pastor is capable by himself of animating the prayer, the song may still need animation.

Certainly the best support of congregational singing is still the choir —given at least that this choir understands its central animating role and that it is so placed in the sanctuary that it can effectively perform this service. The organ and other instruments also have a decisive role in supporting and animating singing. But nothing can replace a person situated at the heart of the liturgical action who intones the melodies, makes a discreet sign for beginnings, indicates the song to be sung next when necessary. The choir director is rarely in a good position for this task; he or she is justifiably more concerned with the choir than with the congregation, and is often off to the side or hardly visible. To follow *that* leader of song, the worshipper would have to look away from the action at hand. The point is that you simply cannot direct congregational singing in the same way that you would conduct choral singing. It's a different art, and a different technique.

By the way, it is commonly found in liturgical teams that the ministers who are the most motivated to develop their musical and liturgical expertise are most likely to be responsible for congregational singing. In France, for example, formation for liturgical animation evolved out of the old schools of sacred music, which is the training base for the animation of congregational song as well.

An Animator's Experience at St. Ignace, Paris

Over the past 20 years, I have, in effect, served as the animator of the weekly liturgies at St. Ignace, and in numerous other Parisian assemblies. As my conclusion, I would like to describe a typical celebration from the point of view of the animator as I have learned to understand the role.

First of all, I arrive at the church well in advance of the choir and the host of worshippers. I check the organist's folder, which contains all the songs, with the key transpositions, the number of verses, and the times of the preludes and improvisations; I look to see if there are any peculiarities in the day's office. Then I check the mike, the books, my own folder. I try to have a free mind and to collect myself before entering into the celebration. There's nothing worse than the "technical difficulty" that sneaks up on you just when the celebration is about to begin!

While the organ is playing and the faithful are entering the church, I don't participate directly in the active welcome at the doors, but I am there, from the start, like a presence — smiling, if possible.

Five minutes before the beginning of the Mass, the organ stops. At the animator's mike, opposite the ambo, I welcome the worshippers. With a few words, I try to turn their minds and hearts toward the upcoming celebration. I choose the difficult or less familiar songs from the day's program. The purpose is not to "rehearse" the songs, but rather to prepare ourselves to celebrate together with the texts and melodies that will make up our prayer. Often I begin with a verse from a psalm. I read the words; I show how they suggest the link between the first reading and the Gospel, and how their meaning unfolds. I sing the melody (or have the choir sing it, or the organist play it.) I have the congregation repeat it. I try to impart a feeling, to arouse the desire. If I suggest that the words be better enunciated, or the singing be more alert, or slower, louder, or softer, it is not for a reason of musical esthetics alone. It is in order that our prayer will be true and that we can better help each other pray together in spirit and truth. I usually end the preparation with the opening song, and it is time for the Mass to begin.

The organ sounds its prelude; the choir begins singing, or I do, if there is no choir. When it is time for the congregation to join in, I make a clear signal. As soon as they have begun, it is not necessary to continue to beat the measure or gesticulate in some way. It's superfluous, and often annoying. I am not like an orchestra conductor or a choir director. I am the "animator of the common prayer." I have no business attracting attention to myself; my job is to orient the people toward their God, whom they are celebrating, and whose praises they are singing.

One of the aspects of my role that has always seemed especially important is that of regulating the *rhythms*. It's my job, for instance, to "sense" the optimum duration of a song, whether to add a verse in order to obtain a proper climax or to cut a song short to avoid overdoing it. It's also up to me to gauge the *silences*—keeping in mind that individuals interiorize their prayer at different rates—after the invitation to pray, or after communion; to find the right cadence for the transitions between a reading and a song, or the acclamation that follows; between the intention to pray and the sung invocation (by all); between each of the various actions or parts of the celebration. It isn't necessary to rally people, nor to control things too much. The effect of interiority in a celebration (an experience that is prayerful) depends largely on the right rhythm of actions and on this quality of judging the timing in such a way that the music is played at the right tempo or a silence occurs at a welcome moment. Finally, I try to remember and apply the good advice I give to others:

—*Don't sing into the mike when the congregation is singing. It can drown them out, and it's acoustically wrong.*

—*Don't move without a reason to move. This distracts everyone.*

—*Don't keep your nose buried in the book or folder.*

—*Don't make unnecessary gestures.*
—*Say as little as possible and don't overexplain anything.*
—*Never upstage the principal player—be it the celebrant, the reader, or whomever.*
—*Don't be preoccupied with the next item on the agenda. In a word, be totally involved with the action of the moment.*

When it is time for a reading, I listen to it for myself. When there is a pause for silent prayer, I turn away from the congregation and, like them, toward the cross or the altar. I know that my role as animator, whether it demands a technique of presence, gesture, word, or voice, is above all a communication of soul and breath. For that, I must first pray myself, and open myself completely to the action of the Holy Spirit.

II. MUSIC AND OUR PRAYER

THE CHURCH AS A COMMUNITY OF PRAYER

Rev. Godfrey Diekmann, OSB
Monk of St. John's Abbey and Editor-in-Chief of Worship *magazine.*

The Church becomes Church above all by worship and prayer. The very word "Ecclesia," from the Greek word meaning "to call forth from," meant, both in the Old Testament and the New Testament, the people whom God has called in order to give him praise. St. Peter, in his first letter, in words that recall Exodus 19 and Isaiah 43, states clearly: "But you are a chosen race, a royal priesthood, a consecrated nation, a people set apart to sing the praises of God who called you out of the darkness into his wonderful light (2:9). A chosen people, chosen in order to sing God's praises."

And so it is to be expected that in the two famous passages in Acts 2, in which the earliest Christian communities are described, their prayer, and particularly prayer in common, is mentioned as an essential activity of their new life. In Acts 2:42: "They remained faithful to the teaching of the apostles, to the brotherhood, to the breaking of bread (i.e., the Eucharist) and to the prayers."

The Church is the community of those whom God has called, and who by prayer and worship answer him. Fittingly, therefore, the first pictorial representation we have of the Church, in the Catacomb of St. Priscilla in Rome, pictures her as a matron, with arms outstretched in prayer: Ecclesia Orans, or the praying church.

The Church is Christ's body, and we, precisely as Christ's body, are called by St. Paul a temple, a house of worship. Is this perhaps also one of the lessons we can learn from the day of Pentecost, when the Holy Spirit descended upon the disciples as tongues of living flame?

Prayer, worship, is the chief task of the Church. So it is by prayer that the Church becomes ever more what she is. As long as she remains true to her task of prayer, the Church cannot suffer an identity crisis.

Vatican II (Constitution on the Sacred Liturgy, #41) calls such official communal worship, especially in the same Eucharist and in one prayer, the principal manifestation, the chief epiphany — self-realization of the Church. The Church is never so much church as when she prays and worships in a manner in which all actively participate. Such communal prayer and worship, in a very real sense, creates the Church.

And therefore, as you very well know, St. Augustine's famous declaration: they who sing, pray twice. Your vocation as church musicians can only mean that you have been called, by a twofold or double-strength vocation, to be instruments of the Spirit in the building up of Christ's Church. It should be a comfort to you to know that therefore, in the eyes of God (even if not always in the eyes of your fellow worshippers, or perhaps occasionally even of your pastors), you are indeed front-ranking citizens in the Church. Your musical talents are a charism of double power and purpose. So, in the words of St. Paul, I say stir up the grace that is in you.

To return to prayer, Father Joseph Jungmann, in his final book on the history of prayer published in 1978 by Paulist Press, writes: "Prayer is an essential component of the church. And it will not cease till the pilgrim Church will have attained its final goal. But the Church, precisely because it is a pilgrim church, is open to the influences of its surroundings and successive cultures." He might have added: and of its interior developments, and I mean here more specifically its drifting, ever since Constantine's peace in the fourth century, into an ever increasingly clericalized society.

There had always been, besides the official communal prayer of the Church, personal prayer, recited and sung either alone or in a group. And Jesus' saying always holds true, and not only of official prayer: that where two or three are gathered in my name, I am among them.

But with the ever increasing clericalization of the Church, her official prayer became more complex and less accessible to the common faithful. And so there developed, in the course of time and inevitably, multiple forms of popular devotional services, some of them of high quality, others barely avoiding the quicksands of superstition. But they filled a need, the instinctive need of Christian men and women to find common strength in praying together with and through Christ and with the newly experienced additional strength of the intercession of the Virgin and saints.

Vatican II, with its stress on official liturgy, particularly on the Mass, as "the source and center" of all true devotion, has led to what I firmly believe an unintended but unfortunate result: what some have called the monopoly of the Mass. Certainly, it has led to the practical disappearance of almost all the former popular, common devotions. And this, without any doubt, has caused a serious impoverishment of our Catholic prayer life.

Yes, the official prayer of the Church, the Divine Office or the Liturgy of the Hours, was reformed by Vatican II with the expressed hope that it could again become the prayer of the entire people of God—in actual practice, and not just by delegation to priests and religious. But the attempt proved only very partially successful; certainly not as successful as the similar effort by Archbishop Cranmer of England in the 16th century, who produced the Anglican *Book of Common Prayer*. However, the reformed Liturgy of the Hours does contain many new elements of high worth, and evidences some measure of adaption to meet the varying needs of those who pray it. It is and should become ever more so, at a very minimum, a sort of official anthology of the riches of the Church's official prayer, a treasure house from which popular devotions can draw, both for structures and for solid content.

Conversely, any continuing reform of the official Liturgy of the Hours should include a serious study of why popular devotions of the past were so popular. Such a serious, professionally expert study has to my knowledge never yet been done. What were the features of the so-called popular devotions that attracted people and filled their spiritual longings and needs? And that serious study must further include, today, the remarkable phenomenon of the charismatic movement and its prayer meetings. The elements of spontaneity, of simplicity, or repetition that they embody have something valuable to teach us about common prayer. The prayers of the church, whether official or otherwise, are not and should not be in competition with each other, much less in mutual conflict. They are, should be, and ever will be, please God, mutually complementary, and as such should learn from each other. For the same Spirit prays in them both (with unutterable groaning sometimes) and the same Jesus Christ is present, whenever and wherever two or three are gathered in his name.

Banners of all colors and shapes are an "in" thing today. What church have you been in recently that didn't have a banner proclaiming "God is Love"? Occasionally one may even find one that says "God is Truth." But how many of you have ever seen a banner in church with the message: "God is Beauty"?

Yet the true, the good and the beautiful are as it were a sacred, indissoluble triad. Denying or neglecting one, especially when speaking of God, could to some faint extent almost be compared to denying one of the three Persons in the Trinity.

What I am trying to say is that for all these many centuries we Christians have been worshipping the God of truth and the God of love! Perhaps one of the greatest and most needed reforms of the future in Christian prayer life will be a long-overdue conscious worship of the God of Beauty, a rediscovery of the God of Beauty, who can only be worshipped *worthily* by our trying our utmost to worship him beautifully.

I say rediscovery, for here is what St. Ignatius of Antioch, writing about the year 108, tells the Ephesians about how they should pray in common: "Yes, one and all, you should form yourselves into a choir; so that in perfect harmony, and taking your pitch from God [isn't that phrase lovely?] you may sing in true unison and with one voice, as strings of a harp, to the Father through Jesus Christ."

Athenagoras, one of the chief Christian apologists in the second half of the second century, in writing to the pagans of his time, again and again kept insisting that Christians try to worship worthily the God of Beauty. In fact, he argues that the pagan idols cannot be true gods because their statues and other representations are so ugly. (On second thought, that might be a risky argument to apply to ourselves nowadays.)

Celement of Alexandria, in the early third century, writes in his "Exhortation to the Heathen": let us sing to the Lord a new song. That new song, that perfect and most beautiful song is the Logos, God's Word, now become flesh. "And He who is of David...the word of God, despising lyre and harp, which are but lifeless instruments, now makes melody to his Father on the instruments of human beings...beautiful breathing instruments of music; the Lord made Adam and us after his own image. And it is the Word of God, Jesus, who says to us, 'thou art my harp, my pipe, my temple.'"

In other words, the Logos is not just a prose word; he is song, he is beautiful music, he is poetry. And we, his temple, must in this temple, which (as he says in the same passage) is the "universe in miniature," must become with Christ this new and beautiful song, a song worthy of the Father who made us in his own image of infinite beauty.

There was a splendid article in *Sisters Today* on "The Healing Power of Poetry," by Robert F. Morneau, Auxiliary Bishop of Green Bay, Wisconsin. (I hope that, too, may be a sign of the times—a bishop who writes eloquently and expertly on poetry in the service of religion.) He cites an author who says of a Hindu preacher: "For Him, God was the First Poet, and the universe and its creatures were His finest poems."

May I make an application of all this to the use of poetry, especially the Psalms, in our public and personal prayer life. We have taken for granted, for a long time, that the early Church inherited from the Jews and used the beautiful poetry of the Psalms in her own prayer services. But it seems quite well established today that for almost 300 years, Christians did not use the inherited Jewish psalters as prayer but rather as prophetic writings, as proof texts concerning the life and miracles and death and resurrection of Jesus. We don't know for sure, but the early Christians seemed to have thought they could produce better prayer forms, more suited to a Christian people. And so a whole new literature of Christian psalms and hymns developed—some instances of which can still be found in several of St. Paul's letters, the Apocalypse and in a work called the Odes of Solomon.

But by the fourth century, the Church seems to have had second thoughts about her own substitute efforts at religious poetry; she now began to use the ancient Psalm poems, and gave them the prominent part in her prayer life that they have enjoyed ever since. And almost the entire body of her own previous poetic and hymnic literature has gone lost. Who knows? Perhaps it is just as well. In any event, it would almost seem that history is repeating itself in our own day. To speak very personally, I have a number of friends who have left the priesthood, and not a few of them used to complain that they had found little spiritual nourishment in their obligatory prayer life—the Divine Office, with its 150 psalms, so foreign and meaningless and irrelevant to present-day thinking and needs. So they shopped around, trying this and that modern author of "contemporary" prayers. They were really trying to pray. But more than one has since admitted that after all this searching they have happily rediscovered the psalms; that nothing can equal them in depth and beauty, and, wonder of wonders, in personal relevance.

I believe there is a lesson here for all of us, in the critical matter of worshipping God in beauty—the beauty of the psalms, which at the same time is inspired by truth, taught us by the God who loves us. As St. Augustine summed it all up, long ago: "In order to be worthily praised by his creatures, human beings, God [by inspiring the Psalms] has worthily praised Himself."

Igor Stravinsky, in a commentary on his "Symphony of Psalms," put it a little more earthily: "I can only say that one hopes to worship God with a little art, if one has any; but if one lacks the gift, one should at least burn a little incense."

James Hitchcock wrote a book in 1974 that stirred up a bit of a hornet's nest. He called it *The Recovery of the Sacred.* His thesis is that the modern liturgical renewal has lost, to a large extent, the idea of transcendence, of reverence and mystery. And I suspect that many of us, perhaps a bit guiltily sometimes, feel that he is right, for as Rudolf Otto in the great classic of a generation ago, *The Idea of the Sacred,* has made clear: there never has been, nor can there be, authentic religion without a sense of awe, of wonder, of mystery. Formerly it was easy enough for us to achieve that sense of the sacred. The worship of the Church was performed in a strange language and with multiple mysterious rites. It was almost a case of sacred magic. In fact, for well over a thousand years, we had a surfeit of transcendence in our worship. Many of us can remember, for instance, the pious language about the super-sacredness of the sanctuary. It was so sacred, reserved only for male ordained ministers and their male servers, that it was strictly off-bounds for any woman, except for the great day of her marriage (conveniently forgetting the women who regularly scrubbed the sanctuary floor!). But now those all-to-easy props, strange language and often unintelligible ritual, have been taken away; and we're faced with the absolutely necessary task of recovering, the hard way, the sense of the sacred. For without a doubt, casualness in worship is the death of true religion.

I'm going to suggest a means of recovering this essential sense of the sacred that may at first hearing seem like a strange suggestion to make to an audience dedicated to active participation by singing and making music. In our Catholic congregations we have succeeded to some extent in achieving the active participation of our people in prayer and song. I propose that we are now faced by the equally difficult but equally important task of teaching them how to listen — yes, active participation by meaningful, reflective silence.

I had the remarkable experience of hearing Alec McCowen at the Kennedy Center in Washington recite (if that's the right word) the entire Gospel according to St. Mark by heart; without any props, without any background music, hardly ever raising his voice — simply telling the story. The huge audience sat in absolute silence, almost stunned and reverent silence. Active participation? Yes, and many yesses. It was participation so intense and so stirring to the mind and heart, as I, and I'm sure almost all the thousands there, have rarely experienced in our lives.

Perhaps here we have a reason why, as early as Justin in the mid second century in Rome, there was, in addition to the ordained bishop, presbyters and deacons present and functioning at the Sunday Eucharist, a special "reader" who was officially appointed to read the Scriptures, one who could better than the assembled dignitaries proclaim the inspired Word of God, so that the people would really listen, with mind and heart. Let me add, parenthetically, that we can never do enough to train good readers, and that, above all, the celebrant should pray aloud at Mass, as the same Justin already remarks, "to the best of his ability." A rigorous course in public speaking should be made an obligatory requirement for priestly ordination. And the inability to or unwillingness to lead a community in prayer, clearly, convincingly, and with contagious devoutness, should be regarded as a far more serious obstacle to priestly ordination than the absence of one or both testicles—accidental or voluntary! (cf. Simonus Maiste, *De Irregularitatibus et aliis canonisis impedimentis,* Rome, 1585. It was a matter about which learned Church canonists solemnly disputed for centuries.)

For prayer is a dialogue of God and man. And listening to God, to the Word of God, is prayer, by far the more important part of prayer. Mary, the sister of Lazarus, sitting at the feet of Jesus, and listening to him, had chosen the better part. And it is almost inconceivable to think of Mary, the Mother of Jesus, as being a talkative person, even in prayer. Instead, the Gospels repeatedly and pointedly speak of her as "pondering what she heard in her heart." But when she did speak, with what unparalleled force and eloquence did the Holy Spirit speak through her lips, for instance in the Magnificat!

One more far more significant experience comes to mind. I am a Benedictine monk of St. John's Abbey. For forty years of my monastic life, we got up at 4:15 every morning and then spent two hours and sometimes longer in church, desperately trying to keep our eyes open, and we called that praying. Now we spend hardly one third of that time in the Morning Office, but I think all of us are happy. In fact, we are eager to come to Office, whereas formerly it was an onus, a burden to be borne in holy obedience. Now we are convinced that we really pray three times as well in a third of the time. It is another instance of the architectural principle of Van der Rohe: less is more!

For now we recite or sing the psalms, leisurely, deliberately, reflectively. We savor the words, giving the heart a chance to catch up with the thoughts our lips are uttering. And we have a period of silence after every Psalm, after every reading, in which (to use a figure of speech much loved by the Fathers and found already as early as about year 130, in the so-called Epistle of St. Barnabus) to chew the cud, or in more elegant language, to "ruminate." There is only one word to describe it all, and it's a word that is instinctively and invariably used

DIEKMANN: *The Church as a Community of Prayer*

both by ourselves as well as by visitors: it is all so much more *prayerful* now. It's probably the best thing that's ever happened to us at St. John's, as a community of prayer.

Active participation. One is almost tempted to exclaim (in hindsight) "What sins have been committed in your name!" It has taken some time, and experience, to learn that there is hardly anything more distracting than what can so easily become a constant babbling of words, however sacred. The new liturgy now actually has rubrics, ritual directions, also for the laity. And that, in itself, is a memorable and highly significant first. And among its directions are specified times of silence. I believe we have, unfortunately, scarcely begun to exploit their meaning and spiritual value; to make of them periods of creative stillness!

But what has all this got to do with your task as pastoral musicians? Much! It has especially to do with your better understanding of your specific function and ministry, within the total context of liturgical and communal prayer. But more concretely, may I illustrate all I have said by applying it to what is often regarded as something quite minor today: namely, the Responsorial Psalm after the first reading.

One of the incontestable (and perhaps surprising) facts about early Christian prayer is that the people, the congregation, were not expected to, and did not, recite or sing lengthy prayers or songs. They "actively participated" solely by acclamations, and in the case of psalmody and hymnody, by interjecting over and over again a brief refrain. It was the responsorial manner of psalmody and prayer (such as has now been restored in the Responsorial Psalm of the Mass).

We might say that things are different now, that most people are literate, are able to read the texts of the more lengthy prayers and songs. Granted. But I am deeply convinced that we still have a more valuable spiritual lesson to learn from the responsorial manner of praying and singing. No doubt, it profoundly influenced the understanding and practice of the prayer life of our forebears, making it a model from which we can draw significant profit today.

We are all acquainted with the practice of the Jesus Prayer; we are impressed with the enthusiastic repetition, times without number, opportunely, some would say inopportunely, of the prayer phrase "Praise the Lord" by our charismatic friends—not to speak of the repetitious Hare Krishna shouting of yellow-robed American Buddhist youngsters on street corners. All of us have, in other words, been moved — and perhaps convinced — of the power of a prayer mantra.

But this is "old hat"; this was known and taken for granted, and practiced, and proved a decisive factor in the prayer life of our Christian ancestors well over a thousand years ago. And it wasn't only one mantra they knew and cherished. They had a rich repertory of such mantras (only they didn't call them that), learned in common worship by means of which their daily life could and often did become that walking in the presence of God within them, that loving communion with God involved in "praying always" — without which any true advance in our spiritual pilgrimage is simply impossible.

And the refrains, which were their verbal contributions to the responsorial psalmody of communal worship, and which by constant repetition they learned by heart, and with the heart — these refrains, themselves almost invariably consisting of words from Scripture, became their daily mantras, the affective, often-repeated brief encounters of their hearts with God.

I owe to an article by Father Gelineau a beautiful quotation from St. John Chrysostom of the late fourth century on this matter. Commenting on Psalm 41, Chrysostom told his people: "Listen well to the Psalm, and remember well (i.e., in prayerful reflection) the refrain you have sung here, let the refrain be like the music master's baton, driving home the content of the prayer you have learnt. For each refrain suffices to inculcate and reinculcate a depth of spiritual wisdom" (*Maison Dieu* 135, p. 105).

Do any of us remember the refrain of today's Responsorial Psalm? Father Gelineau, in the same article, also cites a Constantinople collection of such refrains, from which we can also learn. The majority are not only scriptural but also very brief, 7 to 8 syllables (not words!): Kyrie eleison; Praise to you, O Lord; Have Mercy, Lord; Let us praise the Lord; Lord, that I may see....

I personally believe that most of our refrains in the Responsorial Psalm are too long. While our people are frantically trying to remember them, in order to come in again on the cue, they simply cannot pay attention simultaneously to the Psalm content, which the choir or cantor are singing. If I were pastor, or responsible for music, I would not consider it a mortal sin to abbreviate them drastically when need be.

Add to these Psalm refrains some of the great traditional liturgical acclamations, and you have mantras in abundance: the Amen, about which St. Justin was so enthusiastic, and which connotes both "I believe" and "I shall willingly obey or accept," is one of the greatest and most complete of all prayers, because Jesus was in his whole life and being the Amen to the Father, as St. Paul tells us; the Alleluia, which St. Augustine calls the song of the Heavenly Hosts; the two words "Our Father," which are the epitome of the Good News. (It is said of St. Teresa the Great, that when she tried to meditate on the Lord's Prayer she never could get beyond the two words "Our Father," and often fell into an ecstasy over them); or the Dominus vobiscum, which I for one heartily wish we had kept in Latin because of its multiple and rich connotations, which simply cannot all be contained in any single translation in English or any other modern language, for that matter. Walking in the presence of God by means of such mantras, moreover, doesn't merely include *me* and God. It also means, or should mean, greeting His presence in my neighbor. A good practice to develop in meeting someone, therefore, is not just to say a cheerful "Hi." Try adding, in your heart of hearts, as a regular custom, an unspoken Dominus vobiscum. It'll brighten your day and warm your heart, into a more Christian heart.

And finally, this practice of very frequent repetition throughout the day of prayerful mantras—acclamations, responses and responsorial psalm refrains—learned from the liturgy, the Church's foremost school of prayer, will bring about a beautiful unity in our prayer life. It will no longer be the liturgy *and* private prayer, sometimes in uneasy tension; but the Church's prayer, and its inspired words of Scripture, prolonged and echoed in our personal lives throughout the day, the week.

I have tried to share with you some of the thoughts that have been lying very close to my heart, in all these nearly fifty years of speaking on the liturgical movement as first and foremost a spiritual renewal, a new springtime of God's compassionate dwelling in our midst. And so I shall close with the more immediately pertinent words of the late President John F. Kennedy, inscribed in stone on an outer wall of the

The Church as a Community of Prayer: DIEKMANN

Kennedy Center in Washington: "I look forward to an America which will not be afraid of grace and beauty." Which ringing declaration lends itself to ready paraphrase, to our purpose: "Let us work to achieve Catholic congregations which will not be afraid to worship God with grace and beauty." Amen and Dominus vobiscum.

A GOD WHO HEARS

Rev. Nathan Mitchell, OSB
Faculty, Archabbey of St. Meinrad, Ind.

Late in 1978, a Canadian journalist and broadcaster by the name of Nancy McPhee wrote a wonderfully witty book entitled *The Book of Insults, Ancient and Modern.* The subtitle of the book describes its contents as "An amiable history of insult, invective, imprecation and incivility (literary, political and historical) hurled through the ages and compiled as a public service by Nancy McPhee." *The Book of Insults* gives us a generous sampling of the art of invective through the ages — from the scurrilous nastiness of the Latin poet Martial to the urbane fulminations of H.L. Mencken.

There is, for example, Dorothy Parker's apt comment on Calvin Coolidge. When informed that Coolidge had died, Ms. Parker replied: "How can they tell?" (p. 80). And there is Irving Layton's acerbic comment on Prime Minister Trudeau: "In Pierre Elliott Trudeau Canada has at last produced a political leader worthy of assassination" (p. 151).

But of all the practitioners of the art of insult and invective, perhaps musicians are the best. From time immemorial, it seems, music has aroused the most passionate loyalties and the most intemperate denunciations. There was Mark Twain's famous quip about Wagner: "Wagner's music," sneered Twain, "is better than it sounds" (McPhee, p. 33). And who can forget Paul Hume's remarkably effective review, in the *Washington Post*, of a recital given by Margaret Truman in 1950: "Miss Truman," Hume wrote:

is a unique American phenomenon with a pleasant voice of little size and fair quality...yet Miss Truman cannot sing very well. She is flat a good deal of the time...she communicates almost nothing of the music she presents.... There are few moments during her recital when one can relax and feel confident that she will make her goal, which is the end of the song.

(McPhee, p. 34)

Those of you who were alive in 1950 will recall that Margaret's daddy did not appreciate Hume's humor. An angry president—and an even angrier father—Harry Truman replied to Hume in the best American tradition of invective: "I have just read your lousy review buried in the back pages," Truman wrote,

You sound like a frustrated old man who never made a success, an eight-ulcer man on a four-ulcer job, and all four ulcers working. I have never met you, but if I do you'll need a new nose and plenty of beefsteak and perhaps a supporter below.

(McPhee, p. 61)

Well, that certainly gets the point across. What you may not know is that *church* musicians through the centuries have been among the most prominent givers and receivers of insults. The crabby St. Jerome, for example, complained that the church music of his day was "worldly"—and that it was especially hazardous to "the souls of the young people." (Does this sound familiar? One wonders whether things have changed much since the fourth century!) An anonymous Roman ecclesiastic of the sixth century lamented bitterly that the French Christians made "horrid clucking noises and crush the melody to pieces in their throats." Around 1324 or 1325, Pope John XXII felt constrained to issue a papal bull about the quality of music being sung in churches. Somewhat sarcastically, John distinguished two categories of singers: those who are both skilled musicians and competent singers, and those who merely possess "agile voices." These latter, John objected, are like "drunkards who manage to make it home—but can't tell you the road they went home by!" Still later the English composer John Dowland (in the early 17th century) translated some remarks by a German critic who wrote, with blithe disregard for stereotyping,

The English doe carroll; the French sing; the Spaniards weepe; the Italians...caper with their voices; the others barke; but the Germans...doe howle like wolves.

These examples of sarcasm and ethnic slurs are sufficient, I hope, to show that the relation between the church and music has long been a "lovers' quarrel." No matter how you look at it, the historical alliance between public worship and the musical arts has always been an uneasy one. It is hardly surprising, in light of that tumultuous history, that music and musicians have in our own day been the objects of official ecclesiastical scorn. Many a suspicious bishop and pastor have regarded musicians as shady, reptilian people—barely human—who inhabit the perilous margins of respectability. The twentieth century —like the fourth and the sixth and the fourteenth—has had its share of episcopal detractors whose dislike of musicians seems equalled only by their ignorance of music. I cannot resist sharing with you a comment once made by Archbishop Francis Beckman, who was metropolitan of Dubuque from 1930 until 1946. Apparently, the good archbishop was a staunch foe of jazz, jam sessions and jitterbugs. Permit me to quote him as he has been cited in Nancy McPhee's *Insults Ancient and Modern:*

> A degenerated and demoralizing musical system is given a disgusting christening as "swing" and turned loose to gnaw away the moral fiber of young people.... Jam sessions, jitterbugs and cannibalistic rhythmic orgies are wooing our youth along the primrose path to Hell!
>
> (McPhee, p. 34)

Mercifully (one suspects), Archbishop Beckman died in 1948—and his blood pressure was thus spared the shock of the folk-rock tribal musical "Hair" as well as John Travolta's "Saturday Night Fever."

The examples could continue (one thinks, for instance, of certain episcopal reactions to Leonard Bernstein's "Mass")—but by now I assume you understand what I mean when I say that the relation between the church and the musical arts has been a "lovers' quarrel," an uneasy alliance. Respectability has come slowly and sometimes grudgingly to us pastoral musicians. Often enough, we have found ourselves classified several notches below plumbers, sanitary technicians, and gravediggers in the church's official hierarchy of values. Our emancipation has been a long and difficult one. Today, however, there is growing and *grateful* recognition that a pastoral musician is not an accident but a *minister*, not an ornamental bauble but a leader of prayer. We no longer need to apologize for our presence and our leadership in the community gathered for public prayer and praise. But we all know that emancipations — this one included — are followed by hard years of reconstruction. It is one thing to "free the slaves"; it is quite another to insure that those who have been freed can find justice, dignity and respect for their integrity. Emancipation is one thing; reconstruction is quite another.

It seems that we pastoral musicians today find ourselves in an era of reconstruction. Atlanta has burned; Sherman has marched to the sea; the stillness at Appomattox has erupted into shouts of victory; and Scarlet O'Hara has returned to Tara — a bit chastened, but with plenty of fight left in her. The question facing us is a bit like the questions that faced Andrew Johnson in the 19th century and Jimmy Carter in the 20th: Now that the war is over — now that the campaign has ended — where do we go and what to we do? Wars, whether literal or metaphorical ones, tend, in a paradoxical way, to simplify life: they polarize sentiments pro or con, and compel us to take sides with the hawks or the doves. Peace, the time of reconstruction, is always more difficult to handle — because it forces us to decide where we want to live, how we want to grow, and what horizons we want to explore. The analogy limps, but it does have some bearing on our ministry as pastoral musicians — because we are faced today with a massive task of peaceful reconstruction. A lot of full-scale wars, armed skirmishes and border-disputes have been fought since the second Vatican Council's *Constitution on the Liturgy* appeared 18 years ago. It's time now for us to accept the toilsome responsibility of liturgical reconstruction — of learning how to challenge without being destructive; how to confront without being hostile; how to comfort and affirm without being mauldin.

What are some of the ways we pastoral musicians can contribute to the delicate art of reconstruction? There are three areas in which our ministry is particularly vital for the future.

The first area concerns music as a *constitutive* (*not* ornamental) *dimension* of the liturgical environment. Music is not an embellishment or a "gloss" on ritual activity; it is an intrinsic aspect of ritual activity itself. To put it another way, music is just as essential a part of the environment of Christian worship as presider and people, altar and font, plants and banners, candles and crosses. Music does not "solemnize" worship — it is one of the things that makes worship possible in the first place, just as it is one of the things that makes civilized humanity possible in the first place.

The second area concerns music as a language: a language of gesture and rhythm (my apologies to Archbishop Beckman's ghost!), a language of word and silence, a language of body and spirit. The musician is to the liturgical celebration what the poet is to a people's language. Both poet and musician *minister* to a community's language by keeping old words alive, by exploring new sounds, and by reminding the community that to inhabit a language is to inhabit a history — a history without which past is lost, present is implausible, and future is impossible.

The third area is what I would call the "spirituality of music." Perhaps the phrase is too ambitious and grandiose. But it is important for us to understand the specific and distinctive contribution music makes to the common baptismal vocation of all Christians. Spirituality, after all, is nothing more or less than the gradual unfolding of baptismal conversion in the life of a human being. It is my conviction that just as music plays an indispensable role in our appropriation of humanness, so it also plays an essential role in our ritual appropriation of the Christian mystery through worship. A musician is a person who listens intently for the "speaking" of creation — a person who quests after new sounds, new silences and new voices. Without those sounds and silences, there could be neither poet nor poetry; without the poet there could be no language; and without language there is no human community. In other words, musicians are pretty important people!

Music as "environment." In its recent — and excellent — booklet on *Art and Environment in Catholic Worship*, the Bishops' Committee on the Liturgy states quite unequivocally that music occupies a preeminent place among the arts of public worship:

> Historically, music has enjoyed a preeminence among the arts of public worship, and there is no clear evidence to justify denying it the same place today.
>
> (#6, p. 8)

Preeminence does not, of course, mean exclusivity. The fact is, *all* human environments—including liturgical ones—are thick, teeming worlds of memory, imagination, and bodies that touch, taste, see, smell and hear. Every human environment, however "sacred" or "numinous," partakes in what the Chilean poet Pablo Neruda once called "the poetry of the impure." For Neruda, that "impure poetry" is what makes the human world human:

> ...the holy canons of madrigal, the mandates of touch, smell, taste, sight, hearing, the passion for justice, sexual desire, the sea pounding—wilfully rejecting and accepting another: the deep penetration of things in the transports of love.:..Blossom and water and wheat kernel share one precious consistency, the sumptuous appeal of the tactile....Those who shun the "bad taste" of things will fall on their face in the snow. (Neruda, 1961: 39-40)

Human environments, liturgical environments—like Pablo Neruda's "impure poetry"—are thick verbs full of blood and action. Neruda's poetry celebrates the "precious consistency," the "sumptuous appeal of the tactile"—and he is right, of course. Human environments are relentlessly tactile—and visual—and aural. As John Cage, that honorary leprechaun of offbeat experimental music, has remarked: "There is no such thing as an empty space or an empty time. There is always something to see, something to hear. In fact, try as we may to make a silence, we cannot" (Cage, *Silence,* 8). Cage goes on to describe an experience he once had at Harvard University in an anechoic chamber, a room built of special materials and designed to eliminate all echoes, all resonance and, presumably, all extraneous sounds. In this supposedly soundproof room, Cage was surprised that he clearly heard two distinct pitches, one high and one low. Cage writes:

> When I described them [the pitches] to the engineer in charge, he informed me that the high one was my nervous system in operation, the low one my blood in circulation. Until I die there will be sounds. And they will continue following my death. One need not fear about the future of music. (Cage, *Silence,* 8)

Cage's point—and mine, too—is that all human environments confront us with a rudimentary music—with the raw materials of rhythm and pitch and sound; with the high thin humming of nerves in operation and the low dull beat of blood in circulation. Music begins not by throwing blocks of sound into silent caverns, nor by filling empty spaces with great splotches of chord and melody. Music begins when we become attentive to the voices that are already speaking in an environment. This is why, as every musician knows, there is such an intense and intimate connection between the facts of justice and the facts of bodily life: the relationships of touch and movement, breath and blood, rhythm and repose.

All human environments confront us with a rudimentary music: there is no such thing as an empty space or an empty time. It is essential for us pastoral musicians to remember this fact when we begin to deal with the liturgical environments, the sacred space of a community's celebration. Even before the organist puts a pudgy finger on a key, even before the guitarist picks the first string, even before the cantor utters a note — there is already a "natural environment of sound" in the community's space of celebration. There are no empty spaces and no empty times: music for celebration is created within an environment where there is *already* sound: the sound of the community gathering, the sound of shuffling feet, crying babies, circulating blood, humming nerves, coughs and barks, burps and sneezes, the pounding of rain on the roof and the clanging of bells in the tower.

Pastoral musicians, therefore, have to remember that they are dealing with *two* (not just one) fields of sound — two aural environments — in a liturgical celebration. There is the field of "unintentional sound" — the random barks and burps, the convulsive sneezes and sputters. On the other hand, there is the field of "intentional sound" — organized sounds, rhythms, and pitches that constitute *music* in the ordinary sense of the word. *Both of these environments together constitute the "musical space" of a celebration.* There are no empty spaces and no empty times. This is why it makes a *difference*, musically and liturgically, whether the community is prancing around the parish's asphalt parking lot and waving palm branches — or sitting in a half-darkened church on a pewter-grey December morning. These two situations not only *look* different — they *sound* different. When we minister to a community by planning and playing music, the environment is thicker, denser than our intentional sound of hymns, anthems and antiphons. A congregation of senior citizens obviously doesn't sound the same as a congregation of young families — just as a cello doesn't sound like a French horn, even if they are both playing the same pitch in the same range. In music we call this difference *timbre*—and it's why the unaccompanied cello suites of Bach are probably *not* going to sound terrific on a tenor saxophone. We have to learn to listen to the "timbre" of a congregation, even in its "unintentional music." In other words, we have to learn to listen to the *total environment* of sound that constitutes the musical space of a celebration—and not just to the way Brother Gregory and the other monks sound when we listen to their recordings.

To sum up this point about environment, we need to approach pastoral music the way architects like Mies van der Rohe learned to approach the task of building. Mies van der Rohe realized that a building is not primarily an enclosed space, an object placed in space, it is a living reality that interacts with human bodies; with sky, sun, clouds and rain; with trees and terrain. It is all those things together—building, bodies, skies and landscapes—that constitute the art of architecture. There are no empty spaces and no empty times. It is the same with music, especially music that serves a community in the expression and appropriation of faith. Service music, *pastoral* music, interacts constantly with a larger environment: the unintentional sounds of wind and light and taxis and feet shuffling over brick and concrete. The *whole ensemble*, the *total environment*, is our music. John Cage once proposed that we could compose and perform "a quartet for explosive motor, wind, heartbeat, and landslide" (*Silence*, 3). It sounds preposterous, but of course he's right. Music is not a splotch of sound tossed into empty space—it is the imaginative interaction of intentional (organized) sound with unintentional sound; the imaginative interaction of pitch, rhythm, volume and timbre with the blood's circulation and the brain's humming. As pastoral musicians, we don't merely "plan the music"—we help create and design a total environment for celebration. This is why we need to know not only what the congregation looks like—but what this congregation *sounds* like when it moves, when it sits, when it kneels, when it embraces, when it dances. We need to know the congregation's *timbre*; we need to know how these people sound—and why.

Music is a language of gesture and rhythm, word and silence, body and spirit. The pastoral musician is to the liturgical celebration what the poet is to a people's language.

Most of us can no longer remember the process by which we acquired a language. In a way this is unfortunate, because, as Noam Chomsky has said, by the time we are about four years old we have already performed the single most significant intellectual feat of our lives: we have acquired a very sophisticated mode of thinking and communicating called "speech" or "language." Not only that, but this language is pregnant with inexhaustible possibilities of transformation and creativity. Anyone who has ever dealt much with kids knows how true this is. Children can be phenomenally — sometimes annoyingly — creative with language. They seem to have a preternatural gift for the unusual phrase, the unexpected metaphor, the astonishing twist of meaning. If you don't believe me, take a look at the Muppets show sometime — and listen to the way your kids react to it.

Unfortunately, we spend most of our adult years becoming increasingly *afraid* of language. We settle into predictable patterns — like the occasional grunt emitted over the top of a beer during Monday night football. Before long, our predictable language develops into downright *suspicion* of language: we suspect that language is an elaborate and deceptive scheme designed to entrap the unwary. The result is that language becomes a meaningless, unintentional form of noise for which we feel less and less responsible — and which we use with less and less imagination and precision. Events in our national life — like Ron Ziegler's infamous "inoperative statements" during the Watergate era and the Pentagon's "operation sunshine" (an ornate euphemism for nuclear fall-out) — events like these reinforce our paranoid suspicion that language is a vicious trap, and that we're better off to kill *it* before it kills *us*.

There is, I suspect, a pathological connection between our culture's ability to deal effectively with the world of language and our culture's impatience with the serious demands of music. If Johnny can't read, it may be because Johnny can't speak very well; and if Johnny can't speak, he may not be able to hear very well either. Our collective sensorium seems a bit battered; either that, or our gene pool got contaminated by praying mantises somewhere along the line!

Although this sounds a little facetious, the situation itself is quite serious, because the loss of language means, effectively, the loss of humanity. The *word* is, after all, what makes a human being most distinctively human. George Steiner, in an essay on "Silence and the Poet," has made this point beautifully:

> Possessed of speech, possessed by it, the word having chosen the grossness and infirmity of man's condition for its own compelling life, the human person has broken free from the great silence of matter.... But this breaking free, the human voice harvesting echo where there was silence before, is both miracle and outrage, sacrament and blasphemy.
> (Steiner, *Silence and Language*, p. 36)

To lose language is to lose history, to lose tradition, to lose the vital art of storytelling that makes humans *human*. Why? Because we inhabit humanity by inhabiting a world of language, a world of stories told and retold, of stories reinvented and reimagined, of stories layered with flesh, blood, bone and muscle.

This is why poets and musicians are essential to the human enterprise. Both are story-tellers; both create a world and invite us to inhabit it. Speech — language and word, sound and voice — define the radically ambiguous condition of human beings: for we are simultaneously *defiant* creatures who rival the gods through the power of word, and *articulate* creatures in whom mute creation achieves consciousness, thought, language and song. The word is fire: on the one hand, it is fire we seek to steal from the gods; on the other, it is fire ever-renewed and never-consumed — fire that creates. This is why we constantly need poets to tell us who we are: defiant thieves and articulate creators.

And what the poet is to language, the musician is to Christian people gathered for worship. The pastoral musician ministers to the community's need to know, ever more deeply, *who* it is, *what* it's doing, and *why* it's doing it. Just as the poet "ministers" to a community's language by keeping old words resonant and bringing new ones to light — so the pastoral musician ministers to that language we call "music" by keeping old sounds alive and discovering new ones both intended and unintended. Every poet is both a conservationist and an innovator, a traditionalist and an iconoclast. This is so becuase the poet's job is to resist the death of words, the death of language: to paraphrase Dylan Thomas, it is the poet's task to "rage, rage against the dying of the light." The death of language is the death of a community — and the poet struggles against such death both by guarding a tradition and by breaking language open to new and unexplored possibilities.

Conservationist and innovator, traditionalist and iconoclast: these words also describe the role of pastoral musicians who seek to serve Christian communities today. In its comments on the relation between liturgy and tradition, the BCL's document on *Art and Environment* has this to say:

> Common traditions carried on, developed and realized in each community make liturgy an experience of the Church which is both local and universal. The roots as well as the structure of its liturgical celebrations are biblical and ecclesial, asserting a communion with believers of all times and places. This tradition furnishes the symbol language of that action, along with structures and patterns refined through the centuries of experience, and give the old meanings new life in our times, our place, with our new knowledge, talents, competencies, arts.
>
> (#10, p. 10)

It is the pastoral musician's task—as it is the task of all liturgical artists—both to conserve and challenge, to transmit a tradition and, at the same time, to assist at the birth of new meaning in our time, in our place. In a sense, the musician's task is even more harrowing than the poet's—because language itself, as George Steiner has written, "aspires to the condition of music" (*Language and Silence*, 43). Poets bring a community's language to the threshold of that condition; they push language to the limits, thrust it toward the precipice where speech plunges headlong into song and words take flight into the free play of musical form. Musicians are the ones who take the plunge over the precipice, we assist the birth of new meaning in mid-flight—and we both sustain and challenge a community's identity by putting into its mouth new language and a new song. The effect is exhilarating, but the price is high—and so is the precipice. But that's the way we serve: we are the mothers of new speech, new language in a community—and like most mothers, we are likely to be told that we didn't raise our children right!

The metaphor of motherhood leads indirectly to what I've called the "spirituality" of music. The "spirituality of music" does not mean the sort of piety generated when a small group sits intimately on a carpet around a coffee table while someone punches a cassette recording of the Weston monks and someone else reads breathy selections from Kahlil Gibran. I'm not necessarily attacking this practice, but it's not what I have in mind as a "spirituality of music." As I understand it, Christian spirituality is not the same thing as therapy or self-help of seminars in aggressive affirmation. Like motherhood, spirituality is an unfolding process, a tough discipline that demands extraordinary energy. The feminine metaphor is especially appropriate here because I suspect that women, more than other human beings, understand the robust requirements of *change*: the intimate changes of the body, the subtle changes of the self, the cosmic changes of season and creation. It is not accidental, I suspect, that in the rites and myths of primitive peoples, agents of change are often identified as feminine. The fire, the earth, the moon—all are archaic symbols, strong *feminine* symbols, for personal social and cosmic changes that produce something fruitful and new.

In this very primary sense, the poet and the musician in all of us is a feminine presence—because both poetry and music are primordial agents of change. Art, you will recall, does not merely "reflect" experience, it *constitutes* experience, it is the *agent* of experience—or to put it another way, art is experience "caught in the very act of self-awareness." This is why the simplest definition of poetry—and of music as well—is "the story of change." Poetry and music tell us tales of change, of the human self as changed and changing. And these stories constitute the *act*, the *experience* of change itself. This is why the creation of art is a primary act of conversion in the deepest sense of that word. Art is the simultaneous act and awareness of a changing self—of a self that emerges from unconscious sources of creativity, of a self constructed through interaction with others, of a self that reaches beyond forms and media into the limitless realm of mystery. Both conversion and art tell us the story of self-transcendence, of that insatiable reaching-out of a human spirit hungry for mystery.

By the very nature of their art, therefore, musicians are people deeply engaged in *conversion*, in reaching-out for mystery. This is why music not only *celebrates* change, it is a *primary agent* of change. (This may also be one reason why Plato wanted to eliminate musicians from his "perfect" Republic!) Like conversion, music demands an inexhaustible potential for change. If music were not capable of being inexhaustively renewed and thus changed in every performer and in every listener, then music would die when its composers do. It doesn't, of course. And this is because, for all its "symmetry in sound," music is basically assymetrical, discontinuous and different from the worlds of random noise that sweep our senses twenty-four hours a day. Music is an assymetrical moment that leaps out toward us from within a universe of constant rumble and racket. This is why musicians have to deal with "two fields of sound": the unintentional sounds that bombard us every moment (the trucks, the taxis, the bulldozers, the gurgles and sputters and sneezes) — and the intentional sounds of music that reach out to rescue us, periodically, from sheer noise. Every act of music, then, witnesses to an act of conversion, change, and transformation; it celebrates the reaching out of humanly-shaped sound from the vast inarticulate thunder and rumble of noise.

Ours is a culture in which visual stimuli seem to be swamping auditory ones. In other words, we seem to be going deaf as a people; our ability to hear and to listen *imaginatively* seems to be overwhelmed by armies of visual stimulation. Thus our carelessness about language; thus, too — I suspect — our inability to distinguish the assymetrical "reaching out" of *music* from run-of-the-mill noise. Musak drifting through the department store and the dentist's office has become "something to do things by"; it is something we "float in," like an amniotic sac, while strobe lights and angel dust flash frantic kaleidoscopic messages through the neural synapses.

Paradoxically, our progressive inability to *hear* has also begun to affect our ability to see. Our visual apparatus is so supersaturated and so artificially stimulated that it "shorts out," leaving us with the impression that most things look the same most of the time. Environmental pollution doesn't help matters, of course. When was the last time, for example, that you noticed how perceptibly *different* sunlight in March looks from sunlight in October? The colors are not the same — and the textures of the light itself are not the same, either.

We are a people, then, with serious auditory and visual impairments. And curiously, *hearing* is one of the ways to restore our *vision*. In one of his homilies, St. Bernard of Clairvaux wrote that "hearing ...will restore vision to us if our attention is...faithful and vigilant" (see Robert Lawlor, "Geometry at the Service of Prayer...," *Parab-*

ola 3 (1978), p. 16). Cistercian architecture of the 12th century was, of course, a perfect example of Bernard's point—because that architecture drastically reduced visual stimulation and created churches that were constructed in such geometric proportion that the body itself responded actively to the sound of singing voices. Those early Cistercian monks, in other words, were given a kind of "acoustical rubdown," a "sonic bath," every time they stepped into the church to sing the divine office. St. Bernard called his churches "geometry at the service of prayer": it was his way of restoring vision through hearing. The Cistercian church, built about 1135 at Le Thoronet in southern France, for instance, is so acoustically sensitive that a pin dropped in the nave produces a full set of harmonic overtones and can be heard in the apse about 30 yards away.

The point here is that we may have something important to learn from those anonymous builders of the 12th century—something important not only for architecture but for spirituality as well. Learning how to *hear* again may help us learn how to *see* again: *hearing* can help restore our *vision*. If Bernard built churches on the principle "geometry at the service of prayer," perhaps we could begin making music on the principle "acoustics at the service of conversion." The phrase may be awkward, but the sentiment is sound. The art of Christian music celebrates the changing self: the self that reaches out hungrily for mystery; the self that reaches out to touch and be embraced by a community; the self that reaches out toward repentance and healing. Pastoral music is more than competent technique and professional integrity: it is those things, and much more besides. Our ministry as pastoral musicians is a ministry of conversion, a ministry in an age of reconstruction, a ministry that hopes to restore *vision* through *hearing*. Like the poets, we are conservationists and innovators, traditionalists and iconoclasts. Like the bards and balladeers of ancient peoples, our songs are of earth, fire, water, new moons and new worlds. Like Pablo Neruda, our poetry is the raw impure poetry of human flesh: ours are the "mandates of touch, smell, taste, sight and hearing." Ours is the sumptuous appeal of the sonic—acoustics at the service of conversion and healing. For we know that our God is not only a God who sees, but a God who hears as well.

SIX MINOR HERESIES IN TODAY'S MUSIC

Rev. Nathan Mitchell, OSB
Faculty, Archabbey of St. Meinrad, Ind.

That every movement toward significant change produces some more or less interesting heresies is commonplace in Church history. The past several years of renewal have produced a repertoire of minor heresies about worship that need to be exposed.

Heresy One: Liturgy is fun. After all, celebrations are fun and the liturgy is a celebration. Ergo, a good liturgy should be a scene of leaping exuberance.

Heresy Two: Liturgy reflects "where we are." Less grammatically, "liturgy reflects where we are 'at'." Liturgy celebrates the here and now.

Heresy Three: Liturgy is salvation. The committed liturgical "planner," an office only slightly less important than that of the bishop, is the Catholic version of the born-again Christian. S/he will one day ascend to God with the documents of salvation (proably a xeroxed "community hymnal") gripped tightly in both hands.

Heresy Four: Liturgy is a happening. Happenings happen without ritual and without symbol. The goal of liturgical reform is to produce a liturgy that can happen anywhere, any time, to anyone.

Heresy Five: Liturgy is produced by theology, much as Zeus pro-

This article is part of a presentation made by Fr. Mitchell at the October 1976 meeting of the Music Committee of the Federation of Diocesan Liturgical Commissions.

duced Medussa. And the best theology is to be found in Richard Bach's *Jonathan Livingston Seagull,* Kahlil Gibran's *The Prophet* and Richard Lessor's *Fuzzies.*

Heresy Six: Liturgy is intelligible—which is to say "obvious." It should aim just at or slightly below the level of prime-time TV or presidential debates.

Like most minor heresies, all six of these contain a germ of truth. No one denies that joy, salvation, spontaneity, theology and intelligibility have something important to do with worship and music. They are values, significant values. But people don't celebrate "values" any more than they celebrate "concepts" or "ideas." People do not celebrate abstractions—even pious abstractions like faith and love. They celebrate people and events that are concrete, specific, particular. What the literary critic Richard Hovey once said about poetry rings true for liturgy and music as well: they "have business with the grass." Liturgy and music, like poetry, deal with human experiences that have names, faces, hands, histories, lines, dots, textures, surfaces, cracks and colors. Like poetry, music and worship seek to lay their hands on what is most concrete, most specific, most real about the experience of human life in the world. Like poetry, worship and music seek to explore the "extravangant gestures of creation," the places where mystery makes contact with the skin, blood, bone and marrow of human history. A culture, a Church that cannot discern the "poetics of the ordinary" cannot sing or dance or tell stories or write poems—in short, cannot *worship.* Like poetry, music and worship have business "with the grass," have business with the "poetics of the ordinary." For the God we celebrate in song and story is a God of the ordinary, a God who has business with the grass, a God who identifies himself with the flesh and history of human beings.

This is the God we proclaim as the "mystery of faith." This is the God we explore in worship and music. John Cage, writing on the "purpose of music" in his *Lectures on Silence,* has said it well: "Music is edifying, for from time to time it sets the soul in operation. The soul is the gatherer-together of the disparate elements (Meister Eckhart), and its work fills one with peace and love " (Wesleyan University Press, 1973, p. 62).

The two basic problems that afflict American Catholic worship and music today are the post-conciliar compulsion to "prove" *to oursevles* our identity as "relevant" Catholics; and the general passivity, the irrepressible boredom of our culture. These two problems are closely related. Thomas Day is right when he argues in his "Music Syllabus of Errors" that contemporary liturgical celebration has collapsed into the search for new symbols of conformity. Banners, tape decks and hymnals may have replaced statues, organs and Kyriales, but the ancient passivity of Catholics at Mass is far from being dislodged. And ironically, the old liberal liturgists of the '60s have become the rigid, calcified tyrants of the '70s.

In suggesting some ways we might work to improve this situation, here are three counter-proposals to the "minor liturgical heresies" so prevalent today.

We can say that liturgy is "fun" only if we are willing to say that the cross is fun. Fun is something people create; the cross is not — and neither is liturgy. Christians didn't invent liturgy any more than they invented poetry, dancing, music or marriage. Liturgy is *not*, in the first instance, something we *plan* like fun or football. Worship is the exploration of a mystery that we receive and acknowledge as gift. Liturgical music is music that acknowledges the presence of mystery in the poetics of the ordinary. Sacred music is not something different from "ordinary," "secular" music.

Music that strains to become self-consciously "holy" winds up being neither musical nor holy. Music that strives to become self-consciously "relevant" winds up being monumentally boring and irrelevant. Good church music is simply good music, period. It requires nothing more — and nothing less — than what all music requires: coming to terms with the mystery embedded in human experience through the ordinary poetic medium of sound and silence.

Secondly, music and worship do more than celebrate "where we're at." They do more than register what's going on in the world. There is an ethics both to worship and to music, an ethics that challenges us to explore a world of life, faith and understanding that is larger, deeper, broader and higher than our present experience. It is not the purpose of either worship or music to confirm the *status quo,* even when the status quo is regarded as progressive, liberal, relevant and praiseworthy.

The ethical demands placed on both worshiper and musician exceed practical items such as resisting the impulse to reproduce copyrighted material (although it is certainly praiseworthy to resist this impulse). What draws both liturgist and musician together in a common ethical quest is this simple fact: both deal with modes of transcendence, with modes of going beyond immediate experience into a mystery that deepens even as it reveals itself.

Christians do not assemble for worship and song in order to belabor the dreary obviousness of the "here and now." They assemble to envision a world of new possibilities.

Liturgy and music are forms of *ritual*, forms of *symbolic* behavior. Rituals and symbols do not merely express, they shape and change and modify human experience. Both liturgical and musical symbols are *provocative*. Provocative symbols compel us toward new vision and new understanding. A provocative symbol is something like a bulldog: it sinks its teeth into our leg and refuses to let go until we come to terms with it. It stubbornly refuses to let us sink back into dull, calcified habits of conformity. This is why good provocative symbols can be repeated over and over again. They remain compelling, gripping, demanding. A good hymn tune can function as a provocative symbol repeatedly ("A Mighty Fortress" is one example of a musical symbol that has functioned provocatively through several centuries of repetition).

A symbol that fails to be provocative—whether in liturgy or music—soon loses both power and meaning. It becomes a "soft symbol," a cloying, sentimental nostalgia-trip that inspires little except navel-gazing. One of the problems we face today in liturgy and music is precisely the trend toward symbols that inspire nothing because they require nothing: no thought, no effort, no hard word. Ours has become the age of the "soft symbol"—and the result is much like what happens to the human body when it is fed on nothing but "Twinkies" and "Ding Dongs": flab.

"Where we're at" simply doesn't hack it, when it comes to liturgical and musical symbols. Liturgy is not an invitation to celebrate our world. It is an invitation to celebrate a kingdom that is to come; to explore a mystery that grows deeper even as it reveals itself; to spread a feast that will be eaten but never finished. To enter the world of worship is not to enter a world of soft symbols, but to confront the taxing, strenuous, vigorous and provocative symbols of a God who beckons us toward the future.

By way of conclusion to these reflections on American Catholic church music, permit me to suggest four principles that may help guide us in a period of transition where the present is chaotic and the future remains clouded.

Principle One: Discover the virtue of throwing music away. Some music dies mercifully young. So let it. The Germans sometimes speak of *Gebrauchsmusik*—useful music, music that is decent and pleasing, but has limited value and duration. Not all music is immortal—indeed, most of it is not. Nor is all music high art—some of it is good craft, and there is certainly room for good craft in the arena of church music. There is nothing wrong with using a decent bit of musical craftsmanship in worship, provided we can discern the moment of its death and give it a decent burial.

Principle Two: Small is beautiful. Less is often more. It would be far better to sing one piece at Mass decently, sensitively, with an imaginative use of instrumentation, choir and cantors, than to subject ourselves to the masochistic pleasure of four lifeless hymns and six miserable acclamations. If the congregation can manage only the "Holy," and if the "Holy" is a good piece of music worth the trouble to learn and sing, then for heaven's sake let's sing the "Holy" and forget about the rest.

Principle Three: Don't listen to everything a liturgist says. In this era of renewed conformity, liturgists have become the new mandarins, the new bureaucrats. Keep in mind that Jesus was not a liturgist; that he didn't exorcize the synagogue, but rather the corrosive powers of evil that make people slaves. Keep in mind, too, that the unearthing of liturgical principles is a rather recent form of ecclesiastical paleontology. People were making music long before they were planning liturgies, much as people were writing poems (good poems) long before they were producing literary criticism. The relation between music and liturgy is not one of servant to master, but one of sister to brother. Music is not the "humble handmaid" of worship. Both are modes of transcendence, ways to explore the surfaces of Mystery.

Principle Four: Dare to be unprincipled; dare, even, to be eccentric. Eccentricity is what makes the world interesting. Dare to say — out loud — that the place of both music and worship in Christian life is humble, modest. Dare to believe that music, as a craft and as an art, is likely to survive, even if we don't. Dare to admit that worship, as a response to mystery and gift, will give way to vision. Time is long and so is God. He will continue to unfold himself in history and among people long after our hymnals, sacramentaries and missalettes have become a curious footnote in somebody's doctoral thesis.

Above all, in this continuing time of transition, dare to acknowledge that we don't have all the answers and that we don't even know all the questions. Keep in mind the words of the modern musical eccentric John Cage: "When asked why, God being good, there was evil in the world, Sri Ramarkrishna said: 'To thicken the plot.'" Let's keep the plot thick.

TWO BECOME ONE:
PERFORMANCE AND PARTICIPATION

Rev. Paul Philibert, OP
Faculty, Department of Religion and Religious Education, Catholic University of America.

Each one of us brings all kinds of unspoken expectations with us to worship. Inner-city prophets want to see proclamation and preaching unpack powerful demands from the word of God for justice, mercy and community. High Church types seek musical splendor — brass choir and timpani supplying driving syncopation to the swell of massed voices. Theologically sensitive partisans of "renewal" want most to see all individuals in the assembly open their mouths and *join in*. Still others look for "mystery," the "presence," the sense of the ineffable associated with the age-old sacrifice of the Mass. Most of us represent a blend of these and other attitudes.

While none of these orientations is "wrong" in itself, each one carries a different emphasis in the balance between reason and feeling, word and rite, participation and performance. Inescapably, in common prayer, we exist in a tension between a pole that represents *quality* and a pole that represents *shared responsibility*. Thorough exploration of this question can uncover a balance between these two poles.

One issue seems to be more fundamental than others in getting a perspective on the balance in question. Older generations seemed to relate to the Sunday experience in terms of being filled up: taking their empty human shells to church, they received grace. But so much of the new theology has helped us perceive that this is only half the story.

The other half can be glimpsed in various phrases in the documents of Vatican II: Christ enlivens the baptized through the gift of the Spirit; this Spirit animates "all their works, prayers, and apostolic endeavors, their ordinarily married and family life, their daily labor, their mental and physical relaxation"; and all of this is offered to the Father "along with the Lord's Body," (Vatican II *Constitution on the Sacred Liturgy (CSL)*, #34). Thus, the meaning of the Sunday assembly is not alone that of bestowing the worshippers with holy gifts; it is just as fundamentally a privileged moment in which to testify to the Holy Spirit that is in them.

It is clear from constantly repeated instances that the enormous reluctance of many Sunday Christians to engage in any deep or challenging participation in worship through song, gesture or spoken word is rooted in a preconciliar vision of worship. "Look! Get on with it," they have said to me, either directly or in so many words. Get on with it: Say the Mass, give me the sacrament, fill me up and leave me alone. It is one of the real sadnesses of this period of renewal that there seem to be bishops and priests in the American Church who are content to do just that. And so worship in spirit and in truth — characterized by freedom and joyful urgency — seldom emerges.

There is tension between the liturgy as God's gesture and the liturgy as the believers' gesture. Theologians have long asked, "Is the liturgy formative of community or does the liturgy presuppose a community of believers?" In a certain way it is both. As the activity that hands on to a new day the stories of God in Jesus and the sacraments that he guided the Church to elaborate in his name, the liturgy is formative of community. Any community that no longer accepts these gifts cannot really be called Christian. But the acceptance and celebration of these gifts by themselves do not satisfy the *full* point of the liturgy. Prayer is not so many words read, pages turned, songs sung, gestures enacted, symbols used, sacred objects touched, and so forth. These actions alone are not liturgy, but merely rite. *Liturgy* is lived and living dialogue of human beings with divine beings and among one another — a dialogue that perpetually has the power to make unforseen demands.

When this dialogue is lost, rite easily becomes ritualism. Ritualism by itself can become idolatrous, if for example, an individual were more concerned with observing certain rites than with meeting the living God manifested in those rites. Such observance worships the worship forms, not the living God, and thereby merits the name of idolatry.

Christopher Kiesling attacks our culture's "consumerism" as the force perverting our worship: "The consumer regards liturgy as a product or service to be received, rather than as an event which he or she is to create with others" (*Worship* 52:4, July, 1978, p. 365). The "consumer" doesn't understand participation—and often doesn't have very high expectations of performance either, although the "consumer" *perceives* Mass as a performance. "Participation vs. performance" may signify the gap between turning pages in a missalette on the one hand and experiencing an awesome event of artful prayer on the other; but even more fundamentally, these words express primary realities of Christian experience.

"Participation" expresses first of all the reality of a community of people together. Unlike the Hindu shrine, the Buddhist zendo or the Muslim call to worship, the Christian assembly is not simply a gathering of individuals to make their personal prayers in a common place. The Christian mystery is the mystery of a people.

The idea represents an impressive challenge for all of us. Yet this is the revealed plan: This earthly plane will be transformed. It is a task not for occasional religious heroes, not even for a hidden God alone; rather, it is a task for those called to it—called to achieve the mystery God has preached in Jesus Christ. This means that the Sunday assembly has got to have a pragmatic air about it. The gathering of the assembly has got to be something more than the exorcism of a fear of the mortal sin of nonattendance. It is time for challenge, recommitment, practical assessment, bonding together for the struggle.

"Performance," in the context of liturgy, does not occur in a personal vacuum—as a kind of esthetic eruption without a context. "Performance" is measured and judged precisely in terms of being a response to a preliminary initiative of God within the Church. Yet when God speaks within the Church, it is on the lips of living men and women. The meaning of the measured yet abundant beauty that invests our words and gestures with glory and power—the meaning of "performance"—is that it is the garb of the holy, of that which is most authentic. The words of the Gospel, like the songs of the believers, are not messages for our reasoning minds alone. They are words, gestures and melodies, repeated through the centuries, that create an environment that fosters commitment, pushing us beyond the surface of our fears and providing us an alphabet for hope. We are in continuity with ages of hope.

The community is called to hear the prophetic word of God in the scriptures and to receive the word as a vision for life. Yet no single reading of the word exhausts its power, no single preaching exhausts its meaning. We barely scratch the surface in our celebrations. The prophetic word of God is *expansive*—it unfolds in silence. So many biblical images of God's power are clothed in silence: the Spirit brooding over Genesis, the stillness of Elijah's encounter with God on Mt. Horeb, the midnight birth of the savior, the watching in the upper room until Pentecost. And the silence is followed by an explosive and creative transformation of the world that flows out of the power of the word grown to its fullness in stillness and waiting.

There are many voices of silence. One of its vestures is music. Max Picard claims that music is an extension of silence: "The sound of music is not, like the sounds of words, opposed but parallel to silence. It is as though the sound of music were being driven over the surface of silence." We need to experience this power of music to unlock the hidden senses of the prophetic words of worship—the power to unravel the tangled strands of meaning that underlie words of faith and prayer.

For the word of God to be *life*, there has to be an inner speaking by God that testifies to the saving power of the Church. This inner voice is the anointed silence that unwraps the meaning of the sacred words for us. Most of us have known occasional moments in which the brilliance of a preacher, the touching beauty of a choir's singing, or the magnetic unity of a congregation caught up in enthusiastic song touched something very deep inside us. It is foolish to run away from such moments—to treat them lightly. Like Mary in Luke 2:19, we need to treasure these things and ponder them in our hearts. What is unutterable in the mere toil of words remains real for the heart in the region of silence. Without this silence, holy words can be information, but not salvation.

PHILIBERT: *Performance and Participation*

What we mean by secularity today is not a *rejection* of God, but rather an *affirmation* of God as penetrating the whole of life. It is the assertion that there are not two worlds, one small holy one where God dwells in a golden tabernacle and another large secular one where humankind has unbridled sovereignty. It is the affirmation that there is only one world in which the one God is met in creation, in prophecy, in loving encounters and in the compassionate rebuilding of the earth — and all of this is summarized and proclaimed in liturgy.

To be what it really has to be — the gathering up of all the fragments of life — our liturgical prayer must confront our eyes and ears with an authentic sense of what is churning in the continuing creation of the world. Even if we do not know how to obey God's voice in its midst or how to interpret his message within it, nonetheless God is present in it all. We are too quick to dismiss the changes of the world as unsuited to divine communication, too quick to dismiss God's surprises in our world as unsuited to good taste. If history is any lesson, however, God will not be easily domesticated by our categories of tastefulness. He will dance and make new songs, he will find new media and stick with them until they shine with the rewards of skillful discipline. And if we wish to dance with him, his joy will be the greater.

From these perspectives, it is reasonable to assert that the tension between excellent performance of rites and fullsome participation of hearts is healthy and inescapable. We have to do the best we can to realize both dimensions; both are integral to genuine worship.

In Christian worship, we are called to express our personal gifts fully and deeply, but in the context of and for the sake of a community of varied personalities. We are called to repeat in a new age and language and culture the old stories and relive the old memories, but to do so with freshness and creativity so that they live with an unpredictable power. We are called to challenge one another with the vision of a coming age of justice and love that at present lies beyond our reach, but to do so within a celebration of thanks that so much of the coming age has already touched our lives. To realize these demands, we need to learn how to express a plurality of seemingly contrary values: solidarity/conviction; searching/simplicity; creativity/fidelity.

The creative disbelief of Nietzche in the last century has helped many theologians understand the dialectical tension within which the contemporary worshipper stands. This is representative of Nietzche's challenge to the Church: "For me to believe in their redeemer, Christians would have to sing better songs, and they would have to look more redeemed." Such a complaint helps us see that the tension between performance and participation cannot be collapsed; they must be melded. Performance — the excellence of singing and saying and doing — and participation — the individual's surrender to the transforming work of the worshipping community — must coalesce. One without the other can only be either estheticism or boosterism. Together, they become the enfleshment of a mystery that remains age after age both challenge and promise, surrender and consolation.

III. MUSIC IN THE LITURGY

CHOOSING MUSIC: NO SMALL TASK

Tom Conry

Tom Conry is a pastoral musician, liturgist and composer in Beaverton, Ore.

Perhaps no aspect of the pastoral musician's ministry is so critical in the long run, or as frequently misunderstood, as the selection of repertoire. It has finally become generally accepted that a professionally trained pastoral musician is an asset to the community's faith life. *Deo gratias,* more and more parishes are beginning to allocate reasonable sums for salaries, education, instruments, and so forth. The struggle for quality is clearly being won by the good guys, in apparent contradiction of Gresham's law. Having fought the good fight and emerged victorious, many of us are now faced with that dilemma so endemic to revolutions, what to do when you've won. To slip out of the political metaphor, once the tools for good liturgical music are available, the problem becomes learning how to use them.

Up to now, we seem to have taken the whole question of repertoire in a rather cavalier fashion. We will hear a song from "somewhere" — the radio, a friend, a neighboring folk group or organist — and immediately add it to the body of our musical literature, usually either because it says something "really neat" about "the theme," or because we think people will sing it, and this is what we take as the ultimate yardstick of success or failure. These criteria have both obvious and subtle limitations.

It should be immediately apparent that we are not at all likely to obtain an adequate sampling of what is available in the field — still less an idea of the state of the art — by relying on sheer fortuitous circumstance in coming across good new music. Nor are music publishers necessarily reliable in this regard; they may be helpful, but after all, they are in business to make an honest dollar and usually can be counted on to behave accordingly. The bulk of their advertising budget goes to material that is commercially salable on a broad scale, rather than to that which is critically excellent. This is not to say that the two do not often enough coincide. It is simply that music publishers are in business and we are in church.

One problem in the search for good new music is that so much of the first couple of generations of music in the vernacular has already exhausted its usefulness. The days of fat, romantic major-seventh chords extolling vaguely pious values of peace, love and brotherhood are giving way to more profound, more sophisticated song about what it means to be Christ for one another. Fatuous sentiment is out; honesty is in.

Nor is "the people will sing it" a particularly good bottom-line rationale for selecting music. It is a value — even an important value — but it is not in itself the desired end result. The attitude is probably rooted in our own insecurities; if people sing, then we are positively reinforced. We are demonstrably doing our job; the pastor and parish council are pleased; and God is praised, which nobody can deny, which nobody can deny.

There is a tremendous temptation implicit in this line of reasoning. The truth is that any competent musician can get any congregation with a pulse to sing with reasonable vigor on any given occasion. All we'd have to do is drag out a few of the old anthems (folk or traditional), perhaps add a safe, major-key fanfare — on special occasions rent some brass — and presto! instant participation. It will happen regardless of whether the theology is dated or contradictory, the melody is trite or the lyric is obscure. When a rock group gets low audience response, it turns up the amplifiers; when we're in trouble, we reach for "Crown Him with Many Crowns" or "Holy God." In the long run, though, this is unsatisfying. If we are serious about our art, our ministry, we will come to see that safe, convenient and certain are not enough.

To determine what *is* enough, where we can go for our music and on what criteria to base our decisions, we have to accept the fact that we will not find our music all in one place, listed with any one publisher or recommended in comprehensive fashion in any magazine or book. No single hymnal is likely to contain it; nor is any one composer likely to embody completely all the needs of a particular celebrating community. This adds up to a substantial commitment of time and energy on the part of the pastoral musician.

What should we look for? How will we know good music for celebration when we find it? By now we should be familiar with the musical, liturgical and pastoral judgments set forth by the Bishop's Committee on the Liturgy in their landmark document *Music in Catholic Worship (MCW).* (If you are not, stop reading this article, go immediately to your phone and order it from NPM Resources or your local Catholic bookstore). As an adjunct to *MCW's* parameters for musical, liturgical and pastoral integrity, we can ask ourselves the following questions about our music.

Is it coherent? The text should do something more than rhyme. It should convey a harmony of belief and maintain a common vector with the rest of your program. If you are a devotee of "Humbly We Adore Thee," or "O Lord I Am Not Worthy"—what Ralph Keifer has labeled the "lo, I am a wretch" school of eucharistic theology—then to sing such songs within the context of a celebration of how terrific the community is reduces your credibility. This is not to argue for ideological purity; only for avoiding flat-out contradiction.

Is it intimate? Do we say things to one another about how we really feel, our highest hopes, our most profound doubts, our darkest fears? Are we able to say things in the assembly that would be difficult to say elsewhere, making that space a liberating one? Or do we depend on the rather banal, comfortable distillations of the popular piety?

Is it just? Does the text contain sexist or otherwise chauvinistic references? Is it infested with neo-medieval triumphalism? Or rather does it exhibit a mature generativity; does it turn our attention to the real problems of injustice and selfishness, reminding u of our soc ?tal obligations?

Is it challenging? Musically, is the melody strong and beautiful, or merely trite? Textually, does it call us to consider new ideas, to re-examine our lives? It is about conversion?

Is it truthful? Does it really convey our set of beliefs? Is it about the God we believe in? Or is it unclear, laden with ambiguous and obscure imagery and outdated theology? Worse yet, does it disseminate out-and-out lies?

Is it rooted in the community? Does it identify us in relation to God and one another? Does it name us really as we are or would like to be? Or is it full of "God-talk," that second language of cliches and well-worn phrases that focuses somewhere "out there" and keeps God distant and unreal?

Even within these rather stringent directives, we will in time be able to identify much more of the really good stuff than any community could assimilate. Moreover, in a profoundly hopeful sign of the Spirit with us, more and more quality material is being turned out. The process of deciding what portion of it is appropriate for our community undergoes three stages of growth, the third stage of which outlines a possible strategy for arriving at a program of liturgical music for a parish situation.

The first stage seems to be bounded by what the music director already knows, what the people already know, that is, for the most part, what is in the hymnal or the missalettes. The only thing this has going for it is convenience. Popes may die, kingdoms may fall, great music may be written; in this primitive stage we are musically oblivious to all. In it the musical caliber of our celebration is reduced to the least common denominator: material that has been accepted practice in the past. An anonymous entity, removed from the parish in question, is deciding the content of your liturgical music. You either grow out of this or stagnate; there is no growth within this stage.

The second stage is characterized by a commitment to a discrete, week-to-week thematicism, to the involvement of more people in the process — usually in the form of a liturgy committee or some other planning group — and usually, an effort to match up songs with the "theme" of the Mass.

Compared to the first stage, this model has several virtues. It aspires to coherence. It does not see the liturgy as something to "get through," but rather as an opportunity to make a statement. Further, it recognizes the principle of multiple ministries by separating, at least to some extent, the roles of planner and musician. Although they might be played by the same person, they are understood as two distinct processes. In this stage someone on the parish scene is actively looking for new music or is at least passively aware that it exists and might under some circumstances be used.

Despite the strengths of this model, it has at least two major weaknesses. First, it is often loosely based on a faulty understanding of the liturgical year, and, in particular, the lectionary. The idea seems to be that the people who set up the lectionary (again, that anonymous "they") set things up so that there is one theme for every Mass of every cycle. It revolves around the points of intersection among the three assigned readings. "They" did not get around to telling us, however, what "the theme" was, so we read the selection much as we would a detective story—looking for clues to the elusive theme.

This often takes the shape of scanning for a common vocabulary. For example, if all three readings mention the word "vineyards," we then announce that—eureka!—the theme is vineyards. The next step is to ask the pastoral musician for any songs s/he may know about vineyards. And so it goes, until next week. We probably all recall from high school English that a theme is identified in the form of a complete sentence. The point is not "vineyards," but what we want to say *about* vineyards. It is the *idea* we sing about. Moreover, sets of readings are designed to give us broader access to the richness of Scripture. There was never a theme in mind for every Sunday; rather there exists an imposing array of themes that can be drawn from any set of readings. The universality and variety of the Word is its very essence.

The second difficulty with the discrete thematic approach is that it tends to fragment the liturgical experience. Typically, there is no direction from week to week, no connection from Sunday to Sunday or any common thread for us to follow. Far from ritualizing the rhythm of our lives, this rhythm is syncopated out of existence. We live from week to week with only the twin peaks of Christmas and Easter to establish where we are. Our boat floats all right, but it needs a rudder and a sail.

The model for the third stage of growth allows us the coherence of the thematic approach without doing violence to the lectionary or leaving us foundering for lack of direction. For want of a better lexicon, we may prosaically dub this the long-range planning model. If we could look ahead, take an inventory of where the community is, initiate dialogue about where we want to go and establish what needs ritualizing in our lives on a concrete level, then we would have the information we need to make decisions about repertoire.

To achieve this, we as pastoral musicians should ask ourselves questions such as: What do we believe in? What are we afraid of? What is special about our communities? What do we need to learn? In what areas do we need to experience conversion? What, on the local level, do we have to celebrate?

Once our perspectives shift to this level, the direction our celebrations will take becomes clearer. It is precisely here, at this stage, that liturgy committees can really minister to the gathered assembly. To thoughtfully consider ourselves in relation to the community is the *sine qua non* of mature celebration. The liturgy committee can create a prayerful, faith-filled space for this. (This is why perhaps we should not be so hard on ourselves at meetings where we "just talk" and "don't get any business done." Instead, we should view it as a sign that the process is trying to happen.)

Note that the direction, and themes, of both liturgy and music come from the community level, not from the lectionary. This is consistent with the role of the assembly as the primary minister of eucharist. Once we have established at the community level who we are and what we have to celebrate — specifically, not in vague generalities — then we can go to the lectionary and harvest accordingly from the richness of Scripture. Instead of trying to simultaneously exegetize, catechetize, and actualize the full capacity of the lectionary each week, we can focus our energies on the one or two things we want to do well. Incidentally, this will rarely result in changing the readings for a given Sunday. Once we begin this process, the Word comes alive with new possibilities and new ways of thinking about things.

Perhaps we should do this in a spirit of more concrete anticipation. Plan out in May, for example, what will be celebrated in our communities for the next liturgical year: How will we celebrate next Advent and Lent? Do we need to catechetize about reconciliation? What about the rest of the sacraments? What about Scripture itself — are we still struggling along with a fundamentalist interpretation of the

Word? Can we make it more vital? How about a series on death and dying? Bishop Dozier of Memphis asked parishes in his diocese last year to spend time considering Matthew's gospel; what makes it unique? Why was it written? If we know what we are celebrating, we can begin to find and own (in a musical and legal sense) the music that will reinforce the community's direction and that will encourage it to be increasingly Christlike.

This is not "managing the Word" any more than rehearsing seriously is not letting the Spirit work. The Christian experience is so full of meaning that to insist on swallowing it all at one time is to functionally make the decision to go hungry. God's word and God's eucharist will always be, as Oosterhuis says, "greater than our hearts." We can never truly own this — but we can make it more and more a part of our lives. The best way to do this is with a direction, saying clearly and honestly who we are, one step at a time.

Harry Chapin has written a song, "Dance Band on the Titanic," that may be the ultimate nightmare of a metaphor for us as pastoral musicians; to be playing music, totally oblivious to the sinking ship, our sole function to distract attention from impending disaster. We are not artists to anesthetize; we are artists to sing what is strong and beautiful and true, and to call our brothers and sisters to sing this way. It has been this way for all art and all artists since anyone can remember; and isn't strong, beautiful and true what worship is about, anyway?

SETTING THE TONE

Rev. Robert J. Dufford, SJ

Member, St. Louis Jesuits

Why plan liturgies at all? Wouldn't it be better to simply have everyone come and pray and sing? "Some of the best liturgies I've ever been part of were spontaneous. Planned liturgies seem so contrived, so mechanical." "This person reads this; then this person does that. Then we all sing #28, verses two and five...sort of like a computer program." Or, "the only people that got anything out of it were the people who planned it." "Besides, it takes too much time."

How true many of these criticisms are! Yet most of the problems stem from poor planning — one person types up a list of songs for the next two months; or a three-hour knock-down-drag-out session is spent deciding who's in control; or a business meeting results in a liturgy that seems strangely like a business meeting.

What does it mean to "plan" a liturgy? The backbone of planning is simply to take time *beforehand* to look forward to what is to happen in the liturgy, to anticipate the gathering of the community so that the moments spent in celebration will be richer. The immediate result of the plan should be some point of focus — "a unity drawn from the liturgical feast or season or from the readings..." (*Music in Catholic Worship,*" No. 11). Once determined, this focus can begin to develop within the minds and hearts and talents of those involved in preparing the celebration.

The advantages of taking time and energy to plan are many. Since the congregation usually comes from many psychological outlooks

Setting the Tone: DUFFORD

and concerns, there is a great need for unity of focus to allow them to gather themselves together into community. Often the ministers (celebrant, lectors, musicians, etc.) never get around to praying because of busy-ness. Good planning provides the opportunity for making decisions about particulars *before* liturgy begins, and communicating these decisions to the people involved. This enables everyone to integrate what they are doing into the whole.

Should every liturgy be planned? Based on this understanding of "planning," yes — meaning that there should be some focal point to integrate the experience of those present. Otherwise, the liturgy becomes a series of recitations and movements that congregations will be inclined to consider either magical or meaningless. On the other hand, planning need not imply long hours of meeting and typing. The nature of planning depends on the organizational structure of the worshiping community.

Planning should normally be done by a team of people with different roles and talents. The Bishops' Committee suggests: "the priest (celebrant and homilist)..., men and women trained in music, poetry and art, [with] knowledge in current resources in these areas...[and] sensitive to...scripture, theology and prayer...[and] some members of the congregation who have not taken special roles..." (*Music in Catholic Worship,*" No. 12).

Gathering such a group regularly is often difficult because of their other commitments. Since the concern of this larger group is the *overall* mood and theme of the liturgy, they need not deal with all the specifics. For example, this group need not decide each of the songs to be used, but might give suggestions appropriate to the mood and theme. At a later time, music personnel can select music, remaining faithful to this basic spirit, and communicate their decisions to allow other members of the group to incorporate a sense of the music into their own areas of attention. If the selections do not seem to make sense to the others, they can always ask about them. The music people should be held accountable for their choice of music. Competence in planning music will develop only if there is accountability along with constructive feedback (positive and negative) from others.

"Coming up with a theme statement" is a goal of most planning sessions. While this, in theory, is the unity of focus at the heart of liturgical planning, in practice, concentration on theme only can be restricting for the planning of music. Liturgical music, like all music, is bound up with human emotion: it flows from feeling and evokes feeling. ("Feeling" here is not opposed to or separate from understanding and freedom. Rather, it provides a context in which understanding and freedom can develop in a deeper, more involving way.) "Music" imparts a sense of unity to the congregation and sets the appropriate tone for a particular celebration. Music, in addition to expressing texts, can also unveil a dimension of meaning and feeling, a communication of ideas and intuitions which words alone cannot yield " (*Music in Catholic Worship,* Nos. 23, 24). If feeling is such a dominant factor in liturgical music, then the method for selecting music should be concerned with the feeling or tone or atmosphere of the celebration. Liturgy planning can be much more fruitful if done in terms of "mood" than in terms of "theme" or "main idea."

Consider what happens in your own planning group when you ask, "What is the theme going to be?" Do group members start giving little explanations and moralisms? Do people work mostly at resolving differences in how to word things? Does the group try to write the homily? Are differences resolved by trying to hammer out a more and more general theme statement to cover all the ideas presented? The problem might not be so pronounced in your case. However, a process like this can easily lead to a very wordy, vague, or superficial experience when it finally reaches the total community at liturgy.

This is not to say that "themes" or "ideas" are unimportant or tend to make a liturgy vague, but that a process oriented toward words and ideas alone more easily produces a liturgy that fails to touch people's hearts and is soon forgotten. Moreover, it can present a real problem to the musician who then feels bound to come up with songs having the same words or ideas.

A planning session that is focused primarily on mood might be used by the music people alone or by the more general planning group (celebrant, lector, homilist, musician, other artists). The main point of the first, rather structured, phase is to obtain a sample of the community's response to the liturgy to be planned.

Once everyone is present and hellos are said, a leader calls the group to an atmosphere of prayerful reflection. People quiet down,

Setting the Tone: DUFFORD

consciously relax, focus on what they are about. (An atmosphere of busy-ness can turn planning a liturgy into just another meeting or task, and destroy the entire dimension of living faith.) Someone might pray for the help of the Spirit of God among them to use minds and hearts, feelings and talents for the service of his people. The leader then recalls the general liturgical context (e.g., season of the year, Confirmation Sunday, Thanksgiving, etc.)

Someone reads the first reading, prayerfully, without hurrying. The others simply listen, not following along in another book. The reader pauses briefly to allow each one to recall key moments or feelings evoked by the reading. Then the Responsorial Psalm is read, perhaps with the group repeating the response. Pause again. Then the Gospel selection is read as before. (If there are three readings, the second is not read until later.) Pause once again.

At this point, the group goes around twice: the first time, each one points to the place in the readings that meant something to him or her; the second time, each tries to give expression to the moods and feelings that he or she felt during the readings. The leader (celebrant, if possible) then attempts to summarize and asks if his summary was faithful to the group's experience: "Does this get to the basic things I heard from the group—both the moods and the parts of the readings that moved you?" When there is agreement on this sense of the group, someone reads the second reading (if there is one). If this reading fits with the summary, fine; if not, the group is at least aware of it. (The theory here is that the first and third readings and the responsorial tend to be coordinated; the second often is not). At this point, group members may bring up special events that are already planned. (For example, someone is going to be baptized. It may be fruitful to ask if the group finds any predominant imagery or symbolism—the Lord as Shepherd or King; the Prodigal Son; light and darkness; a tree planted by living water; and so on. Since images and symbols are also bound up with feeling, they too can help express the overall mood.

By the time the group has come in touch with moods and imagery, a statement of theme is usually forthcoming. People are bursting with ways to state the theme, most of them supported by the commonly shared mood. Problems associated with disagreements about wording are bypassed. The individual talents and gifts of presider, lector, musician, and others are freed to find their own expression in harmony with the group's basic experience. When specific decisions are made about songs, homily, visuals, and so on, this information should be communicated back to others in the group. In this way mutual cooperation can stimulate and support the creativity of all. For example, the choice of a particular song may spark an idea for a banner or slide presentation. Or, the specific words of a banner or a key phrase in a homily may help decide which of two or three songs might be more appropriate.

Actually, this format for planning does aim at establishing a theme. The key difference between the approach just described and asking "What is the theme?" is this: consciously, from the beginning, the reflection process involves more than putting words and ideas together. The hope is that when the entire community experiences the liturgical celebration, they too will find more than words and ideas, they too will be moved to receive the Word more openly.

Those responsible for selecting music (or other groups) might use this method effectively as well. The music group responsible for the midnight Mass at Creighton University in Omaha uses this approach at their Wednesday evening session before practicing music. After following the structured process described here, the group is asked to fit and support the mood/theme we have just tried to express. As each person makes a song suggestion, he or she also is ready to elaborate on its connection with the mood/theme. Often the group will sense the connection and agree immediately. Occasionally, someone will suggest a selection that doesn't seem to fit. When asked to explain the reason for the choice, the individual often presents a new facet of the same mood that no one else had considered. Often too, however, in trying to express the reason to others, he or she will recognize that the connection isn't really valid, or the song appropriate.

After completing a list of suggested songs, the group positions them within the flow of the liturgy. Up-tempo or "big"-sounding songs are preferred when more active participation of the congregation is desired, typically at the beginning and end. (Although occasionally for some special reason, the liturgy may start in silence.) There are other, more reflective times when slower, meditative (possibly solo) songs are better; for example, at the response to the first reading (replacing

Setting the Tone: DUFFORD

the read responsorial), or during a collection, or during Communion. Replacing the Responsorial Psalm is a delicate matter. This is a moment when the song must be carefully thematic (aligned with the readings), attentive to mood, and not too long. When selecting songs from the list, it is important to see how many new songs are involved. More than one or two is usually too much for an average congregation. (On the other hand, with music written in antiphon-verse style, the congregation needs only to learn a short antiphon before beginning to use the song.) When a final list is chosen, practice begins, planning at the same time exactly what arrangement will be used, including: who will sing what verses; when to add harmony; which verses to sing strongly, which to sing quietly; when to use violin and flute; which verses to keep ready in case there is a need to fill more time; how to begin and end each song.

Planning liturgy in this way develops within the planners a real sense of prayerful participation. The musical side of liturgy (planning as well as execution) is part of their faith-life expression, not just another job or performance. Moreover, the prayerful attitude of the musicians and singers can greatly affect the whole atmosphere of a liturgical celebration. If *they* have a sense of the overall mood/theme development, the rest of the community will pick it up, even without a verbal explanation. The music itself speaks.

It would not be honest to ignore the possible problems with this method. For one thing, many people don't seem to know how to identify themselves. Some reinterpret the question about mood to respond in terms of explanations and discussions: "I feel that Jesus is telling us that we should..."; "I have the feeling that we must always be ready for death." People often need a facilitator or leader who can draw their attention to the ways in which a reading or prayer *moves* them. People need to see someone else doing this and then to practice doing it themselves. The leader must do this consistently week after week until a habitual sensitivity is developed within the group. Such a person is not always easy to find. Yet without proper leadership (by someone with liturgical savvy, too) and some form of accountability, even this process can become an exercise in doing "whatever we feel like doing."

One last picture: the priest, lector, musicians, and other ministers are present ready and "warmed up" with *nothing* to do for at least three to five minutes before the liturgy is to begin. The planning has been done so that the various ministers have the psychological space to recall the dynamic of the celebration. The musicians have practiced and arranged as much as they can foresee. Mistakes will probably occur—guitar strings may break, organ chords may be missed. But whatever happens now, planning is behind us; this is the way the People of God will pray today....

BEYOND THE SPECTATOR SACRAMENTS

Ken Meltz

Director of Liturgy and Music, Paulist Center, Boston, Mass.; member, Boston Archdiocesan Liturgical Commission.

Imagine three scenes. The first is a Sunday morning at church. The portable baptismal font tells us that there are going to be infant baptisms today. As the service begins, some in the congregation crane their necks to watch as the infants and their parents are welcomed at the back of the church. The Litany of the Saints begins after the homily; some in the congregation mumble: "Pray for us." During the renewal of baptismal promises, most watch but few respond to the ancient profession of faith. We are left wondering: "Is this really our faith, the faith of the Church, which we are proud to profess?" The members of the assembly primarily watch what is going on among presider, parents and infants; *active* participation is elusive.

Now the scene shifts to a Wednesday morning at St. Adelaide's parish. As the family and casket of the deceased enter the church, a combination organist/soloist intones Deiss' popular "Yes I shall arise and return to my Father." Later the assembly mumbles through a Responsorial Psalm. The congregation is not invited to sing. Its sung parts are relegated to the one soloist who is out of sight. The primary motif, like that of the baptism, is one of watching: watching the casket; watching the family; watching the carefully manicured funeral directors.

For the final scene, it is Saturday morning at St. Pancreas parish.

Beyond the Spectator Sacraments: MELTZ

It is a wedding celebration. As the processional begins, most people in the congregation direct their gaze toward the bride, who is gracefully walking down the center aisle. Others, closer to the front of the church, prefer to watch for signs of nervousness in the groom, who is making anxious asides to his best man. Members of the congregation are lined up single file along the entire length of the church, so that they can see the bride enter and the bride and groom leave the church. That they will need binoculars to watch the rest of the ceremony is not a concern. People are largely inert, passive—liturgical voyeurs, if you will. *Active participation* as any kind of reality will have to wait until the wedding reception later in the afternoon.

Do these scenes sound familiar? Have you ever been part of a congregation at such a baptism or funeral or wedding? Have you ever tried to accompany or act as leader of song at such a liturgy? If so, you have experienced a *spectator* sacrament. Typically, a spectator sacrament has three distinguishing characteristics. First, the assembly is primarily looking on and watching rather than acting. Like Peter Sellers' Chauncy Gardiner, they "prefer to watch." Second, from the musical perspective, people are loathe to sing. This clearly leads to a great deal of frustration for the pastoral musician who takes his/her pastoral ministry seriously. Finally, it can be said that a spectator sacrament is primarily an exercise in passivity for most of the liturgical assembly. The goal of this discussion is two-fold: first, to analyze some of the factors that contribute to the phenomenon of the spectator sacrament, and then to suggest ways to help remedy this sacramental anomaly.

The first contributing factor is a matter of theology, or, more strictly speaking, of piety: sacraments are still viewed primarily from a privatized perspective. To put it simply, sacraments are still by and large seen as events that happen to individuals rather than as prayerful actions of the whole community. For example, a privatized perspective views baptism as something the priest or deacon does to the infant. The community's presence and participation are not seen as essential. One can only ask: is this why Sunday afternoon baptisms other than the Eucharistic assembly are still so frequent and popular? The *Rite of Christian Initiation of Adults (RCIA)* goes a long way to offset such a privatized perspective. There, initiation, from beginning to end, is seen to involve the larger community of the Church in evangelization, catechesis, prayer, apostolate and public ritual. But the communal view of initiation set forth in the *RCIA*, which many including Aidan Kavanagh see as normative for Christian initiation, has still not filtered down into the realm of infant baptism.

Now consider funerals. While the funeral liturgy is not strictly speaking a sacrament, as liturgy it suffers from the same spectator problems. A privatized perspective would suggest that the liturgy is for the deceased or for the family rather than as a prayerful time when the Christian community comes together to proclaim its faith and hope in the risen Lord.

For priests and musicians alike, the privatized perspective is most often a problem at weddings. We have all had to deal with couples who tend to approach marriage as a very personal, almost private, event. Many who come to us for pre-marriage counsel may not appreciate the broader social and religious aspects of Christian marriage. "You and Me Against the World" is more than a musical preference; it is evidence of a privatized piety carried to a certain extreme. As long as a privatized view of the sacraments prevails in the popular understanding, we will be burdened with spectator sacraments.

While the first factor is largely a question of piety, the second is much more pragmatic. It is the problem of heterogeneity. At a given wedding, funeral or baptism, we have to deal with a diverse congregation drawn from many Christian communities for the specific occasion. This is clearly a problem when it comes to achieving active participation. As we know all too well, there are significant differences from parish to parish, from diocese to diocese, from one part of the country to another, from one ethnic group to another. While some Church communities are musically very much at home with the revised liturgy, others have yet to scratch the surface. For pastoral musicians, this raises the very real question of musical repertoire. Is there a common corpus of church music (will there ever be?) in America from which we can draw to help heterogeneous congregations proclaim their faith in song? This is an issue not only of liturgical style (do we sing Peloquin or Foley?), but an issue that also must take into account regional favorites and original compositions. Of course, there are other factors in addition to common repertoire that inhibit participation in a diverse congregation, such as unfamiliar surroundings and unfamiliar company: these too need to be addressed if the spectator problem is to be solved.

Ambivalent or mixed feelings on the part of worshipers can also discourage people from full active participation and thus perpetuate the spectator sacrament motif. For one thing, we are all at different levels on the journey of faith. Some parents who present their children for baptism possess a rich, full faith and have decided to share this faith with their child from the outset of his/her life. By the same token, at the other end of the spectrum we have friends and relatives whose faith is at a less developed or explicit level. To them, baptism may appear not as a saving bath of incorporation into the Church community but as a post-natal coming home party with pious trappings. How, given these mixed faith feelings, can we expect a resounding profession of faith from the baptismal party? What happens when you hypothetically ask this question of faith ambivalence of the larger liturgical assembly? It is no act of prophecy to state that different levels of faith in any assembly make full participation problematic.

Funerals are perhaps the most poignant example of ambivalent or mixed feelings, because death and its attendant rituals evoke such strong, often conflicting, feelings. There is pain; there is grief, sometimes relief; and there is anger. In recent years, we have come to understand that bereavement is a composite of many moments of varying emotions. How else to explain the crying, the laughing, the reminiscing, the worrying and even the fighting shared by friends and families at the death of a loved one? Along with the human feelings involved in death and separation, a corresponding problem is in the liturgical rites themselves. How do we, how are we to feel? While the *Dies Irae* both in text and melody seems inappropriate today, so are trite expressions of feigned human joy. The funeral liturgy has to sail between the Scylla of painful loss and the Charybdis of trite optimism. On the one hand, we have to face up to the stark reality of death, something that our culture is adept at avoiding. At the same time, while accepting death, the funeral rites must move the bereaved away from despair to a vision of resurrection hope. The delicate balance we have to achieve in the funeral rites is perhaps best expressed in the words of a wise old Italian Cardinal who composed this line for his funeral card before his death: "Weep because it is human; hope because it is Christian." It is only in facing up to such ambivalent feelings in our congregations that we will be able to deal creatively and sympathetically with the phenomenon of spectator sacraments.

Here are three areas of solution for the problem we are addressing: education, planning and music. It should be clear by now that we are in for the long haul in overcoming deeply ingrained attitudes regarding the sacraments. The privatized view of the sacraments described above has a long tradition in the Roman Catholic Church, and it is not easily displaced. We need to teach ourselves and others that the sacraments are actions that involve the entire Church community as well as individuals.

Preparation programs for parents can help show that baptism is more than a forgiveness of sin; that it is entry into a community of forgiveness. Catechumenate programs that follow the *RCIA* are imbued with the power to highlight the communal dimensions of initiation.

Marriage preparation programs can go a long way toward breaking the stranglehold of the privatized perspective. This is especially true when such programs involve married couples as instructors. There, the larger and more ecclesial dimensions of the marriage event can be brought out.

Funerals are clearly more problematic, since the period right after the death of a friend or loved one hardly seems to qualify as the proverbial "teachable moment." Nevertheless, the presence of friends and relatives at the funeral rites is strong testimony that we are all affected by the mystery of death. The support, empathy, prayers and concern shown by people at funeral homes need to be given a liturgical outlet as well.

Finally, while the liturgy is not the place to "educate" people, a good participatory Sunday Eucharist in most parishes would go a long way toward solving the problem. If we make the regular Sunday Eucharist less of a spectator sacrament, all else will follow in terms of initiation, weddings and funerals.

It has been over ten years since the *General Instruction of the Roman Missal* called for pastoral planning for liturgical celebrations. It has been eight years since *Music in Catholic Worship* amplified this call and outlined which people and what factors should be addressed by liturgy planning. Yet, in all candor, we must admit that liturgy planning is still more a dream than a reality. This is unfortunate in terms of the spectator sacraments because some program of planning can help us know the congregation better, which would result in more active participation. Planning helps give the people involved — namely, the parents and sponsors at baptism, the couple at a wedding, and the relatives of the deceased — a bitter appreciation of the communal dimensions of these rites. Planning is no panacea; but it is a pastorally sound remedial step in dealing with spectator sacraments.

It should come as no surprise that the third and final way to dealing with spectator rites is music. We musicians have first-hand knowledge of the effect that music can have on a congregation. It can charge an often inert congregation with the power to become active participants. Music cuts through a privatized piety, a heterogeneous grouping, and even ambivalent feelings. It is of the nature of music to evoke response. Music is the most potent antidote for the malady of spectator sacraments.

Regarding the use of music at such times, here are five practical axioms. 1. Go with the familiar. A baptism, wedding or funeral is not the time to be new or esoteric. 2. Be aware of the possibilities for such acclamations, especially in the baptismal rite. Brief and simple settings will encourage more active participation. 3. Be aware of the potential of the Responsorial Psalm on such occasions. The familiar dynamic of cantor/congregation interplay can help people become actors in the liturgical drama. 4. Try to develop a core music program of responses and acclamations for baptisms, weddings and funerals. In time, our congregations will become accustomed to these. Familiarity, in this case, breeds not contempt but more active and fuller participation. 5. Rehearse. A brief rehearsal before baptisms and weddings is most appropriate. For funerals, music used at the wake service could be repeated at the funeral Mass, thus avoiding the need for rehearsal at the church itself.

PASTORAL LITURGY IS *NOT* IN THE BOOK

Ralph A. Keifer
Associate Professor of Liturgics, Catholic Theological Union, Chicago, Ill.

Perhaps nothing taxes the brain, ingenuity, skill and patience of the pastoral musician more than the effort to find music that is both "pastoral" and "liturgical." Overemphasis on the liturgical as defined by what is thought to be expert opinion can lead to worship that is removed from the needs of real people. But if the liturgical is defined in contrast to the pastoral, the result is a toss-up — you can either choose to be liturgically correct or you can choose to serve the needs of a living congregation.

When the sole criterion is the immediate needs of people, the liturgy is at the mercy of every new gimmick and fad, to say nothing of the whims of whoever has the most power over what happens at the liturgy. "Give the people what they want" is about as pastoral as the ancient Roman policy of providing the unemployed population with bread and circuses to prevent riots.

The problem is not in a conflict between the pastoral and the liturgical, but in our continuing insistence on using pre-Vatican II criteria for post-Vatican II liturgies. One of the changes of Vatican II was in the official definition of liturgy. Before Vatican II, good meant correct, carried out according to the prescriptions of the liturgical books. But since Vatican II, good liturgy is pastoral liturgy. As the *Con-*

stitution on the Liturgy puts it, "More is required than the mere observance of the laws governing valid and licit celebration. It is their [pastors'] duty to see that the faithful take part knowingly, actively, and fruitfully" (#11). And so the liturgy is not what can be found in the liturgical books, but what happens when the local congregation prays together, using the liturgical books, but also their own special planning and their own special ways of expressing their faith.

This means, among other things, that a variety of factors have to be taken into account to determine whether a particular piece is liturgically and pastorally suitable. It is often virtually impossible to determine *a priori* whether a particular musical item is either pastorally or liturgically unsuitable. Beyond ruling out the inherently unsingable or unplayable, the blatantly heretical, the outrageously offensive and the wildly inappropriate (e.g., "Onward Christian Soldiers" as a communion meditation), the suitability of most musical material depends on when the music is used and the musical capabilities of the ministers and congregations.

Appeals from history are not helpful for making good liturgical judgments about music. Moreover, a liturgical judgment is not a judgment about liturgical history. One of the facts of our liturgical life is that Vatican II was highly innovative at certain critical points. The inherited tradition of liturgical music was not a tradition of congregational song. It was something of an innovation to encourage the use of popular hymns at Mass; these were unknown to the classic structure of the Roman Rite.

In any case, historical precedents do not warrant the continuance of any particular liturgical practice. For instance, that the Christians of the fourth century acclaimed the Eucharistic Prayer with a simple "amen" is not sufficient reason for our so acclaiming it today. If it is, then we should go all out and shout it as did our less inhibited ancestors in faith. Or indeed, if our eucharistic practice is to be determined by what they did in fourth-century Rome or sixth-century Alexandria, then why not insist that people come to Communion only after fasting since previous midnight and abstaining from sex for at least three days? These are older traditions than the acclamation of the Eucharistic Prayer with an "amen," and they have stronger roots in our own culture; they are still enjoined by the Catechism of the Council of Trent. Historical judgments are simply historical judgments. By themselves, they give no imperative for the present.

Sometimes, in fact, it is the contrast between historic and current usage that needs to be taken more seriously into account. Most of our hymnody rather literally and woodenly replaced the old proper chants—Entrance, Offertory and Communion, with the contemporary addition of the recessional hymn. There is something peculiarly maladaptive about all this. Lacking the long aisles of medieval cathedrals (which generated the ancient proper chants), most contemporary churches are simply not suitable for processions of any significance. Granted contemporary sensibilities about ecclesiastical triumphalism, it can even be seriously asked whether there is any pastoral point in processions of ministers. At the very points in the liturgy when people are asked to do the most singing, they are busy doing something else—getting themselves settled into place, finding their money, finding their way to and from their seats, preparing to leave. This kind of usage utterly subverts any possibility for people to appreciate song in the liturgy as an event of prayer.

If, then, most liturgical judgments about music cannot be made *a priori*, and if history is not entirely helpful, then what is? A genuine liturgical judgment about music is one that considers the nature of liturgical prayer and the design of the liturgy. Liturgical prayer is not simply the use of set forms of prayer, though it includes such set forms. Liturgical prayer is dialogue with our ancestors in faith, a point of meeting between an inherited tradition of prayer and a people who live in the present. Neither a blind submission to the forms of the past nor an effusion of present needs and perspectives, rather it is an event of listening and expression, where classic text and contemporary song meet to form one communion in prayer. Liturgical prayer is where people who live in the present perform ancient gestures—which is why the liturgy works best when it can be experienced as both speaking graciously for a hallowed past and addressing us in the present with freshness and spontaneity.

The design of the liturgy is consistent with its nature as a dialogue in prayer. It has three basic aspects. First of all, beneath all our rites lies a classic pattern that is essentially the same in all the churches of the East and West. One of the major concerns of the liturgical reform was to clarify this pattern. There are also a variety of secondary elements in the liturgy that have evolved since its classic development. In the Mass, for instance, virtually all the elements of our Entrance Rites are part of this evolution. Finally, there is cultural adaptation. The minute a priest speaks in his own accent, the liturgy is inevitably culturally adapted because he speaks differently from priests in Poland or New Guinea or maybe even Peoria. Likewise, the minute a liturgical planner chooses a hymn, the liturgy has been culturally adapted to suit a particular congregation.

Liturgical judgment, then, is determining whether or not a particular piece of music aids the congregation to participate in such a way that (a) they can experience something of the classic prayer pattern speaking to them while (b) they can experience themselves as involved in what is happening. The music will therefore both serve to interpret the classic rite and speak for the people's sensibilities. Moreover, where possible, (c) music will serve to interpret other, less important aspects of the liturgy, provided of course that it does not subvert the priorities set in (a) and (b).

We should give much more attention to developing robust acclamations that leave the congregation feeling that they have truly welcomed the Lord who speaks in his Word and that they have made the Eucharistic Prayer their own. We should also begin to ask some serious questions about what used to be called the Ordinary of the Mass. We might, finally, question the sense of developing practices such as stressing processional music. If we were exercising good liturgical judgment, our musical priorities would be just precisely the reverse of what they often are in conventional parish practice.

The pastoral and liturgical judgment is not a matter of either/or, but rather a question of both/and. Good pastoral judgment will encourage deeper participation by the congregation in the liturgy; good liturgical judgment will include the pastoral dimension.

MUSICAL, LITURGICAL, PASTORAL JUDGMENTS: NEW SONG, NEW JUDGMENTS?

Rev. William Bauman

Vicar for Education, Diocese of Kansas City-St. Joseph; pastor, St. Stephen's Parish, Kansas City, Mo.

The sounds of worship are not in the books, engraved on paper; they are not on the desks of critics or in the recording studios of the performers; the sounds of worship are not concepts or abstractions or objects. The sounds of worship are the dynamic, pulsating vibrations of a living people. They exist but for a moment. They unite persons; they express, share, and build faith. But their duration is eternal in effect and growth. The sounds of worship are the servants of a living spirit filling the created universe.

When I was a lad, about a sixth grader, I first learned that sacred music was in a book. At first it was a little book called "St. Basil's Hymnal." Not all sacred music was in the book, because some choice numbers, such as "Goodnight Sweet Jesus," had to be pasted in the back. In high school, I came across sacred music in a different book, a St. Gregory Hymnal. Finally, in the seminary, I learned that there was the real collection of sacred music, the *Liber*, a thick black book with

This article was presented to the National Meeting of the Federation of Diocesan Liturgical Commissions, Albuquerque, NM, October 11, 1977.

ancient square notation in it. A little book of polyphony seemed to rank along with it when we were able to use it.

But then in the late '50s, a number of "unsacred books" began entering the scene. When we first sang Gelineau's Psalm 22, "My Shepherd Is the Lord," the moral theology professor commented that if we wanted to sing westerns we could go elsewhere, and why bring them into the chapel? But the tide had turned. No book could contain the music to be used in worship. Almost immediately there were psalm collections by Somerville, scriptural songs by Lucien Deiss, and then folk songs by Ray Repp and Joe Wise. By the '60s, sacred music was no longer in a book. Sacred music had spread widely and the new could be accepted along with the old. It was no longer a book; it became a "thing."

That there was a "thing" called sacred music crafted by musicians prevailed all through the middle and late '60s. It had a kind of transparent goodness so that it could be dissected on a laboratory table by the music critics and could be seen and agreed to by all. The exceptionally fine piece could be placed on a pedestal where, theoretically, at least, all musicians could stand and admire it. Those who used it could be sure that they were using good music. This concept assisted us through the polarization that occurred in the late '60s, for we could take music of many different styles, examine it, dissect it, and conclude there was the same kind of substantial agreement (or lack of it) as there was for earlier sacred music.

Then as we made the turn into the '70s, music was neither a book, nor a thing, but a living people's prayer. Music need never be on paper, any more than a homily needs to exist on the printed page. It exists in the assembled community. It exists for a brief moment and during that time that it *is*, it is a gift, it is environment for worship, it is a servant to the liturgy, it is a sound, it is vibrations of a living people. It cannot submit to dissection, for it does not exist long enough. When we think of music today, we do not think of a piece of paper, and we do not think of the nicely shaped "thing." We think instead of a living community making vibrant sounds.

The first vibrant Christian communities whose worship song comes down to us in any significant measure are the 4th-century Christians of Milan. Certainly there was song among the Apostolic and early

Christian communities, but with the rejection from the synagogue and the frequent persecutions, little was recorded for posterity. Musical notation was primitive and almost nonexistent. But in the worship of a living community came songs like the Ambrosian Gloria most of us could begin together by heart today. But the embellishment of the hard-to-sing climactic phrase "Gratis agimus tibi" is from a much later age. Was this the song of ordinary people—or of a monastery, or cathedral choir? There is no question that the basic chant was elementary music of a faith-filled community.

From the 6th to the 9th centuries, the Christian community became two peoples. Graduations of ministry dissolved into a priest-clergy and a passive laity. Sacralization motivated by a sincere concern for the divinity of Christ and a forgetfulness of his humanity gave more and more liturgical function, and therefore musical function, to the clergy group. No longer did the laity anoint their sick, take communion in their hands, carry it home to their elderly, feed the poor, sing their worship, or for that matter regularly approach the holy table of the Lord. Instead of gathering joyfully with Jesus as a community to praise a common Father, the people knelt humbly and worshiped Jesus silently and from afar. They were a new people. Their song was the sound of silence.

Meanwhile two new sets of people emerged to sing worship songs: the monks in their monasteries and the cathedral choirs. While their song was vibrant and faith-filled (at least in healthy times and healthy places), there were qualities to these communities that brought unique characteristics to their song. They were closed, lifelong groupings in which complexity could be mastered. They were sources of progress in theology and history and in the art of writing and musical notation. They became, in the next several centuries, centers for the development of fixed meters, notation, organum, improvisation with secondary melodies over a basic known "cantus firmus," and finally, polyphony in all its glory.

With the emergence of distinct worship communities, a distinction that had been smoldering for 2,000 years burst into bright and lasting flame: that between sacred and secular. It has roots in the Jewish tradition. In contrast to Egypt, where there was a single music for prayer and pleasure, and to Arabia where music was for centuries excluded from worship lest corruption enter, the Jewish heritage separated the music. In the early Church this distinction was relatively unimportant and forgotten. But once there was a sacred and secular community, a clergy/monastery community and a folk community; there were two kinds of music for two kinds of people.

The "folk" were by no means without music. They had their faith, their saints, their customs, their fun songs, their vernacular, their troubadours. The Lord was sung of and praised and popular faith was shared in a music that was not admitted to the cathedral. The folk sang their songs; the clergy wrote theirs. The Latin language brought further separation of people and music. Like any historical trend, it was not absolute. The processionals from 12th-century Paris were songs for "choir and all." The singing of the people was a factor in the development of the "Ars Nova" in the lowlands of the 13th and 14th century, but by and large the songs of worship mirrored the people who were worshiping.

This point was made all the more dramatically evident in the reformation. Without exception, as a new people emerge a new sound emerges. In the 16th century, the chorale sung by a full church emerged in Lutheran Germany. The German language dictated new rhythms; the organ dictated new styles. The ecclesiology dictated who would sing. The same applies to Calvinism and Geneva and the scriptural hymn in the style of the Genevan Psalter. Methodism and Congregationalism brought their own new hymnody — closer and closer to the folk song of that day, for the folk sang it. The Church of England changed ecclesiology little and so its music changed little. In the reaffirmation of the traditional Latin liturgy by Trent, the already outdated art of polyphony was brought to a new peak of beauty and artistry by a Palestrina. At the other end of the spectrum the greatly diverse religious sects from the lowlands brought to our own shores a folk song we now label as "Kentuckian."

The lesson of history seems to be that "new sound" and "new people" go together. Both grow organically out of their past. Both grow together. And as in the work of renewal we are truly becoming a new people we should not be surprised that we are making new sounds. As it is a mark of the Spirit's presence that church renewal takes uncharted and surprising paths, so it will be a mark of the Spirit's presence when God's people worship with surprising sounds.

This historical survey should underlie the judgment we use to evaluate and upgrade music in today's Church, specifically, the threefold judgment in *Music in Catholic Worship:* first musical, then liturgical, then pastoral. It is a good division of judgment — valid and true. While it was dynamic and life-giving for several years, reuniting the divergent wings of the American Catholic Church Music Committee, now it is trapping us, and while the judgment is basically true it can be stifling rather than dynamic.

The *MCW* judgment had its root in a "thing" concept of music. There had to be a stationary, ever-existent, written reality called "good music" that a group of good musicians could sit around and analyze and affirm — thus the musical judgment. There was a vast array of historical theological data yet untried — thus the liturgical judgment. There was a growing people concept, a growing sense of the importance of the psychological and cultural elements of liturgical music — thus the pastoral judgment in last place. These distinctions united us and moved us forward, but they also have their baggage and can hinder us and perpetuate a transitional stage, leaving us standing in a doorway.

Here is a threefold judgment that perhaps has the dynamic to move us forward in the '80s toward a yet newer and better sound for worship. First, liturgical music should be *provocative.* "Provocative" implies that music be alive, effective and strong communication; that it say something, both musically and textually. Good music causes reaction like a good homily; maybe acceptance and approval, perhaps violent rejection, but always challenge and confrontation, suggestion, development. It can whisper or shout but it always communicates. It is not Muzak or aspirin, or Nytol. It is not routine, or too often repeated. It is not a story without a conclusion. It is provocative.

Some examples are Richard Proulx's "Look for Me in Lowly Men" (prescinding from a problem of sexist language, an area where sensitivity has grown rapidly and must continue to grow, this piece provokes thought in a happy blend of melody, harmony, text, movement, strength); "My Son Has Gone Away" by Robert Dufford, SJ; "Gift of Finest Wheat," the Eucharistic Congress Hymn; Marchionda's "Come, Let Us Sing"; pentatonic melodies such as "We Are One in the

Spirit"; Joe Wise's "Christ Has Died, Alleluia."

It isn't words alone, it is sung words that can be provocative. "Provocative" includes "good music" but it puts the measured effect in the lived communication experience rather than on the theoretician's desk.

Second, liturgical music must be *prayer*. While it seems so obvious today, it was not so ten years ago. It is the outgrowth of the pastoral judgment (prayer for *these* people) and the liturgical judgment (fitting the prayer activity of this moment in the rhythm of the liturgy). Fifteen years ago, we were asking "Is it right to sing the Glory to God," ... "to murmer the alleluia," and so on. Maybe some people never did ask these questions and still have to. But for the most part, we are now singing the psalm, or clapping at the offertory, or whatever, and we have to ask "Is it prayer?" Ask this often. Start your next planning meeting with a survey question: "What was the most prayerful moment you experienced in Sunday Mass last month?" This question acknowledges that true liturgy exists in living sounds, not in the notebooks of the planning committees.

Some examples of prayerful texts are Howard Hughes' "May the Angels Take You into Paradise" (Music for Rite of Funerals, ICEL, NPM publication) and Kreutz's beautiful new Magnificat for ICEL. Different texts are prayerful in different ways, and the number of good selections is mounting.

This simple judgment removes us from the danger of a new rubricism. We are asking a question that every Christian can answer—the young, the old, the sophisticated, the simple—and a question they all should be asked. We incorporate and subordinate "Is it liturgical?" and "Is it good music?" in the truer question "Is it prayer?"

Third, liturgical music is *simple*. Here is an important lesson to be learned from history. Historically we can trace a cycle of birth and destruction in every style of music through four steps: there is a primitive and elementary concept; the initial style contains a beautiful simplicity and a simple beauty; the style becomes more complex in the quest of further beauty; rejection occurs when no one comprehends. Chant followed such a cycle, polyphony followed in turn, symphony forms gave way to freer styles, and so on. Harmonies, rhythms and melodies are affected. Harmonies grew so complex in Cesar Franck that one could hardly analyze them; increased dissonance, polytonality, tone clusters and tone rows followed. Even rhythms led to syncopation, to jazz, to irregular, to changing rhythms, to multirhythms. Melodies that once moved stepwise with variety from interesting leaps now jump odd intervals, hard to sing. Yet in combinations such as Lara's theme from Doctor Zhivago, a simple new creation of awkward leaps and unexpected harmonies transcends every cultural difference and is sung and loved by all. In the eclectic style of today, we take elements from each of these extremely complex styles and combine them.

Some examples are Richard Proulx's "Canticle of the Three Young Men" (GIA Publications); Bob Blanchard's "Taste and See the Goodness of the Lord" (Composers Forum). It builds simply and stepwise and is very effective with repetition. The psalm verses have real harmonic interest.

Our church composers need to say over and over again "It must be simple," "It must sing itself." I love the simple beauty of the new music of the St. Louis Jesuits (Dufford, Foley, etc.), but even there a complexity is entering into "Dwelling Place," which most parish guitarists are afraid of. Simple does not mean instant music or music for the musically illiterate. But the question needs to be asked, "Can we achieve a provocative and prayerful beauty without sacrificing simplicity?"

AN AGENDA FOR THE AMERICAN CHURCH IN MUSIC

1. We as the American Church must shift gears if we are to make progress in music. Simply put, we are plowing too shallow a furrow. Before we experience change, serious indepth work in music must replace the shallow. We have moved in the last 15 years through many fads and trends without ever lowering the plow. We put hymns on top of and around a Latin liturgy becoming English. We put "traveling" music to our processions. We learned to sing acclamations. We moved from celebration music to scriptural music to service music.

And we always moved "shallow." We never made real investments of money and personnel at the parish level, at the diocesan level, or at the national level. We must shift gears. If music as a priority hasn't surfaced in 15 years when will it?

2. Undue concern with non-participation and the copyright problem can distract us from the task at hand — to develop personnel resources.

3. Every local community needs the musician's ministry to express its own song, to create it, to enable it. Musicians' ministry cannot be achieved at the diocesan or national level. It must be achieved at the parish level if the folk are again to sing their song.

4. The ministry of the publisher needs to be explored and developed further.

   a) We depend on publishers to provide
   — instruments of prayer that facilitate the new sounds of a new people (not a dialogue with a book, or a celebrant, but rather a dialogue with God);
   — a freeing instrument for sign, symbol, and gesture. (Put it down for a while and celebrate!);
   — a creative instrument (never creating the illusion that our worship music is "a thing, in the book").

   b) We depend on publishers to create and facilitate creation of the music of the people's prayer.

   c) We depend on publishers to own and manage our musical heritage and treasures, but we have to ask if we have entrusted this to them too exclusively, if this in fact is distorting their ministry.

5. Ultimately the Church must own its music! The ministry of creating and owning is not for publishers alone. It belongs to the Church. It must be shared effort. Publishers must be paid to create, but they cannot interfere with the prayer of the people, even of the small parish of 100–200 families.

6. The verbal element of liturgy must be substantially reduced.

We must again hear the word of God and return praise in Eucharist. Rubrically the FDLC can provide direction in the use of environment, gesture, and song in the introductory rites in place of the present complexity of words.

7. Models of the Eucharistic Prayer that involve frequent acclamations of the people (with much less verbose and more concrete presidential portions) should be developed with the help of BCL and FDLC.

8. The need for national and regional centers for liturgy training with strong programs in liturgical music is increasing. Goals and strategies should be set to get us there.

9. Creative efforts are needed on a broad scale to develop music *with* ordinary congregations *for* ordinary congregations. The work of the publishers, of ICEL, and of BCL needs to be increased and given more support.

IV. TOOLS AND TASKS

OUR PEOPLE JUST DON'T LIKE TO SING

Robert J. Batastini
Vice President and General Editor, G.I.A. Publications, Inc., and Director of Music, St. Barbara Church, Brookfield, Ill.

Almost every type of worshiping community in the world includes some sort of musical expression in its ritual, and in our tradition, liturgists and liturgical documents alike continue to stress the value of music in worship. It is rather safe to conclude that music as a part of our worship experience is here to stay. Yet, in his often quoted *Commonweal* article, "A Syllabus of Musical Errors," Dr. Thomas Day states, "Congregational singing (in Roman Catholic churches) is a monumental flop." To a most disturbing degree, this assessment of the present situation can hardly be denied. Merely reporting this reality, however, is of little value unless it prompts us to analyze our failure and to prescribe remedies aimed directly at the nature of the problem.

There is a definite participation crisis in American Catholic churches. What is alarming is that an overwhelming number of people —clergy and laity—seem to be content with the existing liturgical practice in their parish churches, or at best they have developed an apparently permanent tolerance of the situation on the ground that it is hopeless, everything has been tried, and measurable progress is all but impossible. This crisis is evidenced by, among other things, "pretend music."

In a church filled with several hundred worshipers, the commentator steps up to the lectern and introduces the day's liturgy, concluding with something like, "Our entrance song is hymn number 17 on page 46 ... please stand." The organist then begins an introduction, which may or may not give a clue to the hymn, and at a point not always spontaneously obvious, the singing is to begin — usually indicated by the sound of the overwhelming voice of the leader of song, assisted by 100 watts of power and a dozen loudspeakers. Unfortunately, in far too many instances, this is about all that is ever heard: a duet or more often a tug-of-war between organist and song leader! Some well-meaning folks in the middle make an effort to "join" in the hymn, but we rarely experience an entire congregation lifting its voices in song. What is this musical exercise? Pretend music! A whole congregation of sincere, well-meaning people pretending that an entrance hymn has just been sung. Each week the hymns are announced and nothing resembling community song ever happens. This pretense goes on in parish after parish, week after week, as the apparent norm, seemingly unchallenged by anyone in the worshiping body.

On Ascension Day a few years ago I witnessed a classical case. The usual announcement came, asking everyone to please join in the hymn, "Hail the Day That Sees Him Rise." When the organist finished what was a reasonable and rather obvious introduction, nothing happened. No one sang. As the organist kept playing, it was apparent that the congregation did not know the hymn, since not even the typical murmur was heard. To select a hymn for public worship that the congregation does not know is in itself engaging in pretend music, but the real charade came when, with the priest and other ministers already in their places and an entire chorus of nothing but an organ solo, we all pretended our way through the second stanza! Two verses with not even the voice of the song leader — since he, too, obviously did not know the tune. And everyone in the church seemed content with the whole matter, reacting like this was a normal experience.

A year later at another parish on Ascension Day, I sat in a pew preparing for the celebration as the strains of "Mother Dear, O Pray for Me," "On This Day, O Beautiful Mother" and "Mother, at Thy Feet Are Kneeling" wafted through the church in continuous medley propelled by full tremolo — all in preparation for the celebration of Our Lord's Ascension.

More recently, I arrived at still another parish in time to witness the closing song of the previous liturgy. Standing in the back of the church gave me a good vantage point from which to notice that hardly anyone in the entire congregation picked up the missalette when the closing song was announced. It came as no surpise, then, when no voices were heard. It seemed such a meaningless exercise for all those people to politely stand there for one verse of the (non)hymn before leaving.

Often I hear, "Our congregation doesn't like to sing," or "They don't like the songs in our books," or "We have a lot of elderly people, and older people don't sing vigorously" (the same is often said of young people, or this or that ethnic group), or "The lighting is poor," or "People would rather just sit and listen to the beautiful voice of the song leader or to the choir" or "People just prefer to pray silently." If we allow ourselves the convenience, we can rationalize endlessly to explain our unsuccessful attempts at developing congregational song, and we can come to accept these as the causes of an unchangeable condition. None of the standard excuses for poor congregational singing, however, possess more than a minimal degree of validity. There is no such thing as a congregation that cannot or will not sing. An alarming number *do not* sing, but this does not presuppose that improvement is impossible.

Imagine for a moment, Anytown, U.S.A. — a community of about 20,000 people. (Substitute a neighborhood within a large city for a similar analogy.) The town has a Catholic church, a Lutheran church and a Methodist church. Go to the local supermarket, the bowling alley, the department store, the park, and try to tell the Catholics from the Methodists from the Lutherans. Of course, it is impossible and even the suggestion is silly. The point, however, is simple yet important: people of a given community are essentially of the same culture. They work together, shop together, play together, fall in love, marry, raise families and are usually distinguishable by religious denomination only when they publicly worship as Lutherans, Methodists or Catholics. Pursuing this analogy just a little further, you will quickly recognize the Catholics by an absence of the dynamic song that usually accompanies the worship experience of the other two groups.

Why do some Christian bodies sing so vigorously in worship, while Catholics so frequently do not? Tradition? Perhaps, but traditions can be developed. And in more than 15 years we have in many cases failed even to get started. This failure, unfortunately, is principally due to a series of misguided attempts at initiating congregational song, which have seriously retarded or perhaps reversed our progress toward the day when congregations will sing with vitality.

We have witnessed many unfortunate attempts to solve the problem of weak congregational singing. Some have made the mistake of assuming that music in worship must be simple in text and tune, often of not much more than nursery rhyme character. This approach runs the risk of being offensive to thinking adults by at least subconsciously suggesting that the mean literary and musical mentality of people is approximately that of a five-year-old. We have so often assumed that unless music in liturgy is a mediocre form of popular music (almost none are ever of the caliber of the commerical "Top 40" though they directly imitate the style), it is not relevant.

We have made the terribly mistaken judgment that people tire of a tune rather quickly and that we must therefore change the hymns and acclamations frequently and be sure not to use a tune more often than this or that number of times. Some have assumed just the opposite — that congregations either do not like or cannot learn new tunes. They are therefore self-sentenced to a life of singing the same limited repertoire.

Some have mistakenly assumed that "organ" automatically means old music and that only "guitar" can mean "new," overlooking the fact that new hymns in the keyboard idiom are written every day. We have almost unanimously subscribed to the belief that a leader of song, singing all of the congregational music through a public address system, is necessary and even desirable. (Have you *ever* seen a leader of song functioning in such a manner in a Protestant church, where more often than not the singing is exuberant?) We have made the mistake of treating music as ancillary to the liturgy, something for the people to do when the priest is doing something else. We have abused music to the extent of reciting songs: the Alleluia, the Sanctus, the Responsorial Psalm. (How often have you *said*, "Sing a new song to the Lord"?)

We have made the common error of omitting the third verse of a hymn honoring the Trinity, or we have selected hymns that raise a question in one stanza, and give the Lord's answer in another, without singing all the verses. We have generally failed to consider the poetry of a hymn, doing things that seriously abridge the text, affecting the literary intent in such a way as to suggest that the words we sing are really unimportant and that the hymn singing is just liturgical busywork — giving the congregation something to do.

These are only some of the many approaches, techniques, philosophies and gimmicks that are being applied like Band-aids to the problem of the wholly unsatisfactory congregational experience in a majority of the parish churches. And as yet, we have made little or no progress. Some have completely given up, using the earlier stated conviction, "Our people just don't like to sing!" Some, however, are still searching for the right answer, the unlocking of the secret to achieving a church filled with the sound of voices raised in vibrant song.

It can happen! Every parish in the country can experience enthusiastic song in all of its liturgies. It will not necessarily be easy, and it may not be inexpensive, but it is achievable...everywhere!

GOOD ENVIRONMENT HELPS

Environment relates to the general aspects of the worship space, its facilities and equipment. Acoustics are a major factor. In an acoustically "dead" building, vigorous congregational response in spoken word or song is impossible to achieve. What is acoustically desirable in a fine restaurant, for example, where relaxed quiet is valued, is to be avoided as most undesirable in a place of public worship where the people have a definite vocal part in the proceedings.

In a theatre, the audience merely laughs or applauds. A dead room does not interfere with the performance so long as the stage is properly amplified. Although a church may resemble a theatre, with an audience area (the pews) and a stage (the sanctuary), in function there is no similarity since the entire building is stage with everyone having a vocal part in the drama that is enacted there.

Yet so many modern church buildings are constructed with an abundance of interior sound-deadening material. Acoustical tile ceilings and carpeted floors may be attractive to the eye, but they are *always* detrimental to sound. It is sad to witness the excitement in some parishes when special funds are raised, and new carpet is laid, all with the net result of a building perhaps more attractive, but now less suitable for public worship. It would be better if they were to raise the funds and tear out the carpeting and put in tile floors. Within certain extreme limitations, the more echo the better!

Although the ministers can overcome some aspects of a dead building with an adequate sound system, even if microphones are positioned at each place in the congregation (similar to a congressional chamber), the congregation singing in a "dead" building is akin to a piano without a soundboard, a trumpet without a flared bell or a guitar stuffed with cotton. Specifically, the sound amplifying device (for a congregation, this consists of the walls, floor and ceiling of the room) is absent and the musical result is weak, unpleasant, dull and strained. Poor acoustics (no echo) may be costly to correct, but until it is done, nothing will work and even a very large choir or orchestra sounds anemic.

Environment also takes in the matter of the sound system. We tend to be very stereo conscious. It is not uncommon to find a home stereo system costing well over $1,000. We must be equally hi-fidelity conscious in installing sound systems in our churches, if the system is going to serve adequately. If we can easily spend $1,000 to fill a living room with good sound, we had better be prepared to spend a substantial sum of money to equally fill a building that holds hundreds of people. A good sound system, in some ways, is like no system at all; it gives the impression that the speaker or singer is being heard naturally.

Remember, too, that an excellent system for speaking may be inadequate for music due to a limited frequency response. Unless the frequency response is of sufficient range, a guitar may more closely resemble a ukelele, and flute a toy whistle while singers tend to resemble Tiny Tim. Lastly, a well-designed system will channel the sound from the same direction as one's visual perception of the speaker. It is esthetically distracting to have the sound come from the left, right, rear or overhead while the person speaking is in front.

Almost every church or chapel is equipped with an organ, and there are as many different types of organs as there are motor vehicles (e.g., motorcycles, sports cars, compacts, sedans, station wagons, limousines, buses, vans, trucks, etc.). It is important to realize that organs can differ in capacity and function as much as a motorcycle differs from a semi-trailer truck. It can be that extreme. The wonderful, kind and generous gesture from the family who donated to the church the organ that they bought for their living room because no one ever learned to play it (and anyhow, the church needed a new organ) has unwittingly done more to guarantee the failure of the music program than to help it. Put it in the rectory or convent! An instrument designed for a living room can no more fill a church than a motorcycle can haul a ton of freight. It is that simple. Be it electronic or pipe, the instrument must be designed for the size and acoustics of the particular building, or it is totally useless as an instrument associated with congregational singing. Spending much less than $10,000 or $12,000, even for a rather small church, will be wasting money on something totally inadequate.

Regarding pipe organs, lest one think that they are anachronistic, there are more pipe organ companies in business today, and more of these instruments being built and sold today than ever before in history! A pipe organ can last as long as the building stands, and then, if desired, it can be removed and rebuilt in another when its original home meets the wrecker. Any pipe organ technician can repair any type of pipe organ using parts available from numerous suppliers. Electronic organ parts generally must come from the factory, and electronic organ servicers often need to be factory trained to service the specific brand. Pipe organs sound better. The cost of an adequate electronic one (and the good ones are expensive) represents the same potential investment as a good number of pipes. Finally, it does not take a very big pipe organ to do a splendid job of leading the congregation. Six or seven ranks (with the possibility of later additions) can raise quite a joyful noise. Above all, do not rely on the opinion or word of just one or two organ salesmen or organists. Buying a new instrument is a major investment in an item that will have a critical effect on the worship life of the parish for many, many years. Choose carefully.

A suitable environment is critical to living worship. When in doubt, consult; visit other churches with different environmental conditions; compare.

NEW MUSIC: STEP BY STEP

When people refer to the apparent unwillingness of their congregations to participate in song, I always ask about the response to "Silent Night" or "Joy to the World" on Christmas Eve. I ask if patriotic songs such as "America" or our national anthem are rendered with a greater degree of response on holiday weekends than the hymns on the ordinary Sunday. With the usual affirmative reply, often attributed to the "spirit of the occasion," I go on to ask about Easter Sunday, usually to learn that the singing on that day never measures up to the level on Christmas or a holiday. Does this mean that Catholics are more inspired by the Fourth of July than by the Feast of the Lord's Resurrection? Hardly.

What this really means is that every American has grown up with those patriotic songs; it means that we have a significant repertoire of Christmas carols to which most people know at least the first verse from memory; and it means that we do not have a similar Easter repertoire (with the possible exception of "Here Comes Peter Cottontail" and "In Your Easter Bonnet," neither of which have much to do with the Resurrection). There is a definite axiom that the degree of response improves as the people's knowledge of and familiarity with the material improves. We cannot ask people to sing what they do not know. Yet, we seem to attempt just that, and regularly.

We live in a musical swampland. Music plays constantly in our homes, cars, places of employment, the stores where we shop. Television brings constant strains of melody to our ears (even the news has a theme), and practically all nationally advertised products and businesses have commercial jingles, such as ". . . we do it all for you." Our day is filled with the sounds of one kind of music or another; it is in the background everywhere, like the paint on the walls. If a person is so bombarded with melodies day in and day out, how can we expect her/him to remember and sing a new tune after the organist has played it through once? And this is so often done with nothing more than a words-only copy in the people's hands. (Do not underestimate the average person's ability to follow music notation. Nearly everyone is helped somewhat by seeing the visual rise and fall of the melody given in the printed music, and you would be amazed at how many people actually do read music.) In heeding the psalmist's call to "*sing* a new song to the Lord," we all to often ignore the verb. We cannot sing what we do not know!

It is indeed possible and necessary that we develop a repertoire of thoroughly assimilated new music, and it can be done by observing a few simple guidelines.

To begin, less is more. It is far better to introduce a few tunes and to learn them well — so that they have been committed to the repertoire and can be used with confidence in the future — than it is to use a lot of new material, most of which will never be done well because of the congregation's failure to totally assimilate it, and most of which cannot be recalled after a few weeks of not having been sung.

Imagine for a moment that we had really learned just ten new tunes per year since the beginning of the vernacular liturgy. We would have developed a repertoire of over 180 songs by now. Again, less is more. Thoroughly learning just five or ten new hymns per year — seemingly few — will ultimately result in a greater number of hymns that can be selected for use at any time with the confidence that the rendition will be strong.

We must choose new material carefully, avoiding that which is possibly not worth the effort required to fully learn it. If it will not wear over an extended period, or if it is not what we would want to be able to recall at a later time, it is probably not worth doing at all. The fact is that there is far more good material available than any single congregation could ever use in a once-per-week worship situation.

In order to bring about the desired results, it is necessary to introduce the new music to the congregation with a well-planned approach. New hymns need to be introduced in a three-to-five minute session before the beginning of the liturgy. This rehearsal should begin just one or two minutes before the appointed time of the Mass. It is necessary to have the cooperation of the priests, who should readily agree when they realize that this is the only way to develop a repertoire. This rehearsal should be a weekly affair, but should be avoided on Christmas, Easter, Pentecost and other extraordinary days, when a prelude does far more to set the mood for special celebration than the rather pedestrian affair of a music rehearsal would.

The mini-rehearsal is usually conducted by the cantor (song leader) or perhaps the choir director. When introducing the new hymn, avoid using the word "teach." "We are going to learn a new hymn" tends to be more attractive and more community-oriented. Do take a few seconds, when announcing the number and title of the new hymn, to give it some kind of identity. "This is an early 19th-century American hymn, much in the same style as 'Amazing Grace' " prepares the people for what is about to follow. When the introduction of a new hymn is planned well enough in advance, the parish bulletin can carry a paragraph or two about the hymn, information that can easily be culled from a hymnal companion or one of various resource books on hymnody.

The cantor begins the rehearsal by singing the first verse once for the people. (If a choir is present, perhaps it can perform this function.) Next, the cantor sings one phrase at a time, asking the congregation to repeat each phrase in a lining out process. It is all-important that the cantor be sensitive to the response. If the first phrase is repeated poorly or incorrectly, do it again, and again if necessary. Remember, it is not the process, but rather the results that count. Depending on the particular tune being introduced, the singing of the tune once by the cantor and the consequent lining out process may well have used up the alloted time. If enough time remains, however, the cantor should once more sing the whole tune through, and finally, the congregation should try it.

Having done this much on the Sunday on which the new melody is first introduced, it is best not to attempt to sing it in that day's liturgy. On the following Sunday, begin with an invitation to "take another look at the new tune we began learning last week," and repeat the whole process again! Because the tune will ring at least somewhat familiar from the previous week's experience, the process should move along faster, the reponse to the lining out of each phrase should be better, and you should be able to get into the second; third and subsequent verses. Unless the new hymn is complicated and difficult, it can probably be used on this second Sunday of its introduction with a modest degree of success.

The hymn-learning process can be handled in a number of ways. The person introducing the new material can work unaccompanied from the lectern, singing one phrase at a time as previously described; or, the organist can become involved in the process by playing one phrase at a time (melody only—no harmonies); or, the cantor, choir director or song leader can sing his or her part unaccompanied, with the organ leading the congregation on its repetitions of the leader's phrases. In the latter case, it must be remembered that under no circumstances should the leader attempt to lead the congregation in its response. That must be done by the organ alone.

The introduction of new material can be enhanced by the organist's playing of the tune, or of material based on the tune, as prelude or incidental music. While this alone is insufficient as a method of introducing new music, it is most beneficial when used to supplement the learning process.

Singing presupposes the vocalization of words according to a tune. We do not sing solely for the purpose of inspiring the congregation with a catchy tune. And despite the fact that it often appears as though the choice of tune receives more attention than the choice of text, it is in the text that the purpose and meaning of our song is found. Hymn texts are poetic. Rarely are they in a style and form of English that we would consider conversational. Poetry is not conversational language. Poetry is a specialized literary form. A well-written hymn is contructed to convey certain thoughts relative to our faith-experience as a people. In the case of probably a majority of really well-written hymns, it does harm to the message and meaning of the text to abbreviate it by only singing the first two or three stanzas.

We will never, as a Church, mature in our hymn-singing experience until, among other things, we learn to sing hymns in their entirety. Singing all the stanzas has the effect of saying that the hymns are an integral part of the liturgy, and not something we tailor in length to fit the pace of the entrance procession (i.e., congregational busywork). When the celebrant reaches the chair and opens the book to finish the hymn with the congregation (if he has not carried the book and sung in procession), it gives reason and purpose to the song. On the other hand, the practice of regularly ending the hymn with whichever stanza marks the arrival of the celebrant at the altar, regardless of where we might be in singing the message of the text, shouts loudly and clearly that this hymn-singing activity is really not important to the integrity of the liturgy. What we sing has no meaning; getting the ministers in at the beginning and out at the ending is all that counts.

If we do abbreviate a hymn by omitting stanzas, then we should carefully cut out only those stanzas that will leave a remaining text with integrity of meaning. Singing all the stanzas of all the hymns, including the closing song, has the effect of stimulating a greater vitality in our congregational singing by making it obvious that congregational song is important to the total liturgy.

If we are prepared to invest in the building up of a repertoire of music for worship, we will be able to look forward to a day when congregations will know a broad enough selection of hymns to allow us to choose music for specific liturgies with an ever-increasing degree of thematic pertinence. We must be able, however, to look to the future. As the gifted liturgist Regina Kuehn has suggested, we sometimes deal with liturgy as though we were a persecuted Church — worshiping in a tent with the fear of having to pack up and disperse at any moment to avoid an enemy, concerned only with the here and now. We must begin to experience the establishment of a certain type of relative permanence, an investment in tomorrow.

HOW THE ORGANIST CAN LEAD THE CONGREGATION

In order for the congregation to sing well, it must be well led. If symphony orchestras, college glee clubs, high school bands and elementary school choruses (to name a few music-making groups) require the leadership of a competent director, how much more our congregations — those untrained, unauditioned and mostly unrehearsed singers — desperately need a competent leader. And, just as no other musical ensemble ever performs with more than one leader or conductor at a time, it is vitally important that we leave the leading of the congregation in the hands of one person, and one person only. "Hands" is to be taken more literally than it may appear, because the best congregational singing will result when the leading is done by the organist and the organist alone without the aid of the all-too-common "leader of song."

Because the organ (if adequate) is a powerful instrument capable of commanding a leadership position in performance, and because a song leader aided by a sound system has the power to command a leadership position in performance, the use of both results in a *de fac-*

to situation of two leaders. This is totally unworkable, and often the direct cause of the congregation's uneasiness with song. It is very difficult to feel the urge to sing when caught between two strong forces that are not fully synchronized.

By using the proper registration and a number of proper techniques, the organist is fully capable of eliciting an exuberant response from the people in the pews. This, in fact, is the way it is done in those places where congregational singing is best, and this includes the full range of other Christian churches.

The first and foremost rule for the organist is to set and maintain a steady tempo. This must be done regardless of time-delay factors, acoustical problems, the organist's ability to hear the congregation and the congregation's apparent inability to keep pace with the organ. Organists who do not maintain a steady tempo most certainly do so unconsciously. The only way to know whether or not one does in fact maintain a steady tempo is to test oneself. The easiest way to do this is by using a metronome. Far from being a tool for young beginning piano students only, it is very much the tool of the professional. While the young beginner on flute, clarinet or other band or orchestra instrument usually experiences musical ensemble performance from the very early days of his/her musical training, keyboard players can go on for years without ever performing with another musician or musicians. This lack of ensemble experience places keyboard players in a sort of musical ghetto — a situation that yields quite easily to the development of bad musical habits, especially "sins" against strict rhythm and exacting tempo. By using a metronome, an ensemble of two is formed: the machine and the musician. This has the very positive effect of forcing the organist to play with rhythmic precision.

Try sitting down with your hymnal and metronome and play the hymns you used in last Sunday's liturgy. Set the weight at 60 beats per minute, then move up to 80, then 96, and finally 112. If you are unable to accurately play the hymns at all tempos, then *you* are the problem with the singing in your parish. Now don't run off to the rectory and turn in your organ key in a fit of frustration. Rather, use the key to open the lid, get out the metronome and practice, practice, practice. Develop the ability to set and maintain a steady tempo at all costs. If lightning thunders, a baby cries, or an altar boy drops a cruet, you must go on unflinchingly. If the congregation seems to be a half beat, or a beat, a whole measure or even a whole verse behind you, wish them better luck next week, but don't wait for them. Your playing must have the predictable momentum of a professional recording. Then, and only then, will the congregation feel comfortable with your playing and begin to feel as though they want to sing. But beware, fast is not necessarily steady. Steadiness at any tempo is the goal.

The partner to a steady tempo is careful phrasing and articulation. Most hymns appear on the printed page completely without rests. But singers must breathe, and therefore, rests are necessarily implied at specific places throughout the hymn. In order to give shape to the playing of all literature (and for this discussion, hymns), the organist must lift off the keys at the ends of musical phrases, and do so in an exacting manner.

The duration of a note (its time value) is determined not by the strike, but rather by the release of the note. In 4/4 time, a quarter note is released precisely on the second beat. A half note is released at the instant of the third beat; a whole note on the fifth beat. An eighth is released precisely on the "and" of the beat. The note before a rest is released precisely at the moment when the rest begins. Organists' failure to play rhythmically usually stems from their failure to sustain notes for their full value, or from the opposite problem — the failure to get off the note when they should.

If the phrase of a hymn ends with a half note, you must treat it as a quarter, releasing is precisely *on* the second beat for a quarter rest. If the phrase ends with a whole note, treat it as a dotted half and release on four. A quarter note in this position is treated as an eighth note followed by an eighth rest. These pauses must be extremely precise and are best practiced at very slow tempos with exaggerated movements while using the metronome.

The same kind of precise lifting off the keys must be accomplished for repeated notes in the same voice. For example, the first six melody notes of the familiar hymn "Holy, Holy, Holy, Lord God Almighty" are printed as two quarters of the same pitch, followed by two more quarters of another pitch, and two half notes of a third pitch (a "do-mi-so" configuration). In performance, however, the first of each pair of quarter notes must be played precisely as an eighth note followed by an eighth rest, and the first half note must be played as a quarter followed by a quarter rest. Only then will the sound result in something resembling that which is written. Many organ instruction books treat these techniques with a greater degree of thoroughness than space here permits. The purchase of such a volume and its study will result in a wise investment of money and time.

The matter of introductions needs special attention as well. Three common faults in this area are: treating the introduction as an unfortunate necessity (something that delays the actual start of the hymn); introducing all hymns in the same way (such as by always playing the first four bars); and playing an introduction that does not give the singers a clear cue when to begin singing. Introductions must be musical. They should in themselves sound good. They establish the tempo, tonality and melodic character of the piece, and, most important, they set the mood for the hymn. A well-played introduction can do much to stimulate a strong response. A few bars hurriedly rendered in a manner that suggests that the organist would rather not have to begin with this formality, however, cannot do much to stimulate the spirit of song. Effective introductions are almost always an entire verse of the hymn, usually begun rather quietly, followed with a steady crescendo accomplished by adding stops at each phrase to build toward a strong vocal entrance.

The cue for the singers to begin, however, is contained more in what you do *not* play rather in what you *do* play. The cue to begin is given by bringing the introduction to a full close with a slight ritard and a full rest. The singers, upon hearing the organist lift off the keys, will breathe. Allowing the length of one beat in the tempo of the ritard, both organist and singers begin together at normal tempo. The cue must be clear and exaggerated. If the singers do not respond with a strong attack, the rest is probably too short, with the organist's entrance coming before the singers have finished taking their initial breath.

In order to effectively lead the congregation, proper organ registration must be used. This means that string stops, reeds (with some exception using "full" organ) and tremolo are never used. This means that only one or two 8′ stops (a principal, diapason or full sounding flute) are used with one or more 4′ stops (again a principal, flute or octave) and one or more 2′ stops. To that, a mutation, or preferably a mixture, is added. The human voices tend to cancel out the 8' sound. People singing with full voice will not be led by a tubby, mushy or mellow sound. The upper work—4', 2' and II, III or IV mixtures, sometimes necessarily coupled at the 4' level—create the brilliance that the people hear and to which they can raise their voices in fullness. The use of the "pop" effects found on some electronic organs may be novel, but absolutely detrimental to the congregational singing experience. Leslie speakers and any kind of vibrato or undulating effect must always be avoided as tasteless and ineffective. Never use a 16' stop or coupler in the manuals unless you are playing an octave higher. The "fullness" of this effect is really muddiness. Indisputably, a clear, steady, bright tone will best lead the congregation.

What the organist must do in playing for congregational singing is assume the attitude of leadership. Be in control. Play with aggressive authority. Be firm, articulate, strong and rhythmic. Play with the vigor of a drum and bugle corps, or a brass band. Neither rush nor race; be steady and solid.

On the other hand, this type of "in command" playing can diminish an otherwise good performance by choir or cantor. When playing for choir while another assumes the role of director, the organist must be totally submissive to the musical direction of the choirmaster. The choir director must lead and control both organist and choir in a musically precise ensemble, with full confidence that the organist will be responsive to every gesture and direction.

When the cantor is singing and accompanied by the organ, it is the cantor who leads—setting style and controlling nuance. It is important that the cantor feel support from and confidence in the organist. At no time, however, should the cantor feel rushed or pushed by the accompanist. Problems of coordination, tempo, phrasing and dynamics need to be dealt with in rehearsal, and regular sessions for cantor and organists (together) are an absolute necessity.

The ultimate flexibility is required of the organist in cases such as the rendition of a Responsorial Psalm. With a rather quiet registration, the organist plays the refrain as an introduction and then *accompanies* the cantor's singing of the refrain. Instantly changing roles from accompanist to leader and adding sufficient registration (usually accomplished through a manual change), the organist then *leads* the congregation in its repetition of the refrain, allowing the cantor time to breathe and swallow. The organist then again assumes the accompanist role and reduces registration to support the cantor in the singing of the first stanza, and so on. This flexibility is essential, yet usually not so easily achieved. For some it will be necessary to work most diligently to develop the technique and form the mental attitudes. You cannot, however, begin to consider yourself a good church organist with any less a degree of competence.

PRAYER AND MUSIC: SINGING THE MEANING OF THE WORDS

Rev. Mike Joncas

Composer and Associate Pastor, Presentation Parish, Maplewood, Minn.

The first grade assignment for art class is to draw the manger with Mary and Joseph and the Baby Jesus. Johnny includes in his rendition a shadowy figure looking not unlike Friar Tuck: it is "Round John Virgin."

Singing the meaning of the words indeed! Johnny's problem with "Silent Night" is different in degree only — not in kind — from the problem of a congregation invited to sing hymnody whose texts have no meaning to them. Listen on a Sunday morning as our assemblies sing of "bulwarks never failing," "cloven skies," "regal scepters," and "dungeon, fire and sword." In order to squeeze any meaning from such texts, members of a congregation must make gargantuan imaginative leaps.

The musician who exercises a ministry and takes responsibility for what is communicated by means of music in the liturgy must be sensitive to language appropriate to Christian ritual. Specifically, since liturgical discourse is primarily *evocative*, language that is appropriate to the liturgy must call up and identify human experience, recalling and making that experience present in the cherishing of the Word itself. The analogs for such discourse are not to be found in computer print-outs; rather, proper parallels are to be found in poetry and in the silent language of the heart.

Singing the Meaning of the Words: JONCAS

People throughout history have cherished the evocative Word through the medium of music. From native American chanting, through the sustained "om" of Eastern *mantras,* to the jubilus of the last *a* in a chanted "alleluia," music causes something to happen that transcends the content of both text and music. Compare the Easter "alleluia" intoned by a solo voice at dawn accompanied by brass and timpani with a mumbled "alleluia" accompanied by nothing more than the rustle of missalettes. Literally, they both "mean" "praise the Lord" — but their effects are worlds apart. The point is that the meaning is there only when the text is enhanced by music. Ritual music is represented by the convergence of two factors, only one of which is "musical." The most impeccably performed piece of Renaissance polyphony may evoke no more than polite admiration, while the rough-hewn emotion of an "Amazing Grace" may speak volumes of prayer in a cracked and broken voice and rickety piano. Thus, the first task of the liturgical musician is to frame and determine through music the liturgical event that is taking place.

Processional music, for example, is simply accompaniment for movement. This accompaniment may be triumphal (organ *sfz* and a horn quartet *ff*); it may be lyrical, with a solo flute improvising *mp* while a dancer cherishes the holy space; or it may be penitential, with muffled drum and the low chant "Kyrie Eleison." But the music is tied up to the event. It would be silly to extend processional music long after the movement ceases. It is not music done for its own sake. By the same token, an acclamation is a virile shot of musical adrenalin, not a perfumed aural bath. A chant demands a setting that evokes contemplative prayer, not just a perfunctory run-through of the required number of text repetitions.

After determining the nature of the event and the part music is to play — whether autonomous or subsidiary — the musician must consider the text. Again, the discourse generally proper to song texts is evocative and poetic; in Christian ritual we sing *proclaimed* theology, not systematics or rubrical directions. One wonders why we need song to inform us that:

We greet the Lord present within the assembly;
We hear his good news announced clearly to all;

Our priest is presiding; in Christ we are abiding,
As we invoke God's blessing and answer his call.

or:

These 40 days of Lent, O Lord
With you we fast and pray.

Texts like this deny evocative discourse; they report on the present condition rather than call up from the assembly the deepest articulation of what it means to be called to live God's life in the world.

The musician must make a judgment on the literary quality of the text s/he is called to sing or set. All too often musicians simply decide on a song's use from its melodic appeal and a single phrase or two of text that make some vague reference to the liturgical event. We cannot continue to sing doggerel. Admittedly, song-poetry is a different genre than spoken poetry, but the same standards for clean imagery, careful attention to meaning as determining meter, unhackneyed vocabulary and common intelligibility must be applied. But until musicians begin to exercise this critical responsibility, we will be inundated with vague paeans to peace, love and personhood in place of real liturgical poetry.

It is only within this context that the musician can turn to the proper musical techniques for the communication of the texts' meanings. These techniques include tone, volume, timbre, phrasing and accent.

First, *tone*. There is a tone presumably suggested by the composer as well as a tone called for by the text. One does not sing Wagner with the same tone with which one sings Debussy (and this is not just a matter of volume!). Similarly, one does not sing "Jesus Walked that Lonesome Valley" with the same tone one sings "O Sacred Head Surrounded." By and large, musicians have a keen ear for the tone appropriate to various musical genres—how many of us would buy "Tiny Tim Sings Rossini's Greatest Hits"?

We are not as sure of ourselves when it comes to the tone demanded by the text. Our churchly vocalizing falls into the same tone of sanctimony that plagues certain preachers. The only "holy" organ tone is flutes with plenty of tremolo; the only "'holy" vocal tone is transported lyricism, eyes gazing heavenward. Balderdash! A real insight lies in the Old Testament language for prayer: there was no single word for "prayer," only laughing, cursing, singing, pleading, joking, arguing,

Singing the Meaning of the Words: JONCAS

pondering in the presence of God. Similarly, there is no single tone appropriate to all religious texts—some Psalms are angry and should be sung with rage; others, quietly meditative, demand vocal restraint and lyricism: still others are more didactic, or proclamatory, or ecstatic. Tones appropriate to the entire gamut of human emotions should be found and incorporated into the technical repertoire of cantor and choir member.

Second, what about *volume*? Perhaps the key word here is variety. Who says that all the verses of a basically joyful hymn have to be sung at the same volume—one step this side of the pain threshold for our ears? Who says that an instrumental piece played after Communion has to cause Aunt Jane to turn up her hearing aid six notches? Different events and texts call for different volumes; thus the need for a congregational leader who can indicate precisely the volume needed to bring out the meaning of a song. Don't be afraid to experiment with unusual volumes for familiar texts. Clarence Rivers wisely notes in an introduction to his setting of the eucharistic acclamation "Christ has died" that singing the same text, melody and harmony at a restrained volume after the congregation is used to full-throated performance may create an overwhelming sense of acclamatory reference. A certain freedom is needed here to run with the spirit of a given celebration; the liturgical musician will be informed soon enough by his community if the volume does not evoke the meaning of the text for the assembly.

Third, *timbre*. Bernard Huijbers, in *The Performing Audience*, suggests that professional Western musicians may have developed an unexamined cultural prejudice against certain musical timbres. Consider the opera star, incredibly facile in full-throated Italianate vocalization, who reacts with disdain to the timbre of Hank Williams' "Jambalaya." Can any of us accurately reproduce the vocal sounds of a Turkish love song, or the Spanish Passion week *saeta*, or the call to prayer of a Moslem mosque? Perhaps as in the matter of tone we need to be more attentive to the various timbres available to us in the singing assembly—just men's voices (yes, it *can* happen), just women's voices, only children under 10, only teens, only adults over 40, and so on. If we are serious about communicating the meaning of the texts we sing, it's a little foolish to have women lustily belting out "Rise Up, O

Men of God" or a children's choir doing the Nunc Dimittis. We need to overcome our prejudice that the only "real" group-singing timbre is a disciplined choral sound, beautiful as that is. There are timbres expressive of the whole people of God that can only be achieved by untrained voices transforming "Holy God We Praise Thy Name" into a doxology to rival a Schubert "Gloria."

The matter of *phrasing* is perhaps the most difficult of all, especially when dealing with full congregational singing. Any language is more than a discrete package of defined verbal events; the structure of those events determines meaning as well. Thus "woman-without-her-man-is-a-savage" brands the speaker a male chauvinist pig, while "woman — without her, man is savage" will win the speaker the PTA Gloria Steinem Public Speaking Award. Thus the musician must be concerned not only about musical phrasing but the sense of the text itself. Usually metrical hymnody presents the most problems; the obligatory caesura at the end of each half-phrase produces such heresies as "alone we find salvation" (rather than "in your kingdom, Lord, divine, alone we find..."). One solution — invite the congregation and/or choir to *read* the text with you, thus getting its bare cognitive meaning as well as its phrase structure. Hymn writers and composers have not always been as helpful as they might be in avoiding such pitfalls in the communication of meaning.

Finally, *accent*. Here Huijbers is especially helpful in defining the problem if not providing ready-made answers. He notes that the peculiarly Western prejudice mentioned earlier has influenced our modes of transcribing music; purely vocal techniques (including accent) must be forced into transcription schemes that are designed primarily for instrumental effects:

> The variations instruments normally dispose of are: *short-long, high-low, loud-soft, fast-slow*. But how, for example, is one to notate a vocal accent which is not to be sung louder, but by shortening the vowel of the preparatory syllable? How does one indicate a light accent?...[Instruments] are constructed and used for tone-color stability, whereas vocality, correctly understood, is based on tone-color variation.
>
> (*The Performing Audience*, p. 97)

Thus the liturgical musician has to be even more attentive to the literary character of the text, because its peculiar combinations of

Singing the Meaning of the Words: JONCAS

vowel and consonant sounds must be examined to determine precisely the accents and modes of accentuation that will bring out the meaning of the text. Will liquids (l, r) and soft sustained vowels express rage in the same way sibilants (s, x) and clipped, sharp vowels do? Can singers be trained to use the alliterative and onomatopoetic qualities of the text to enhance meaning? (Of course, one is caught up short here when the text is in a foreign language or is a "singing translation" of the original.)

The meaning of a musical event in Christian ritual cannot be divorced from its context. There are times when music and text become so wedded through traditional use that the song-word-event becomes more than the sum of its parts. A recognition of this leads to a certain caution in using the "metrical aids" that have sprung up recently, claiming to provide texts appropriate to every conceivable liturgical event, to be stretched on the framework of familiar hymn-tunes. I am not opposed to this in principle, and often the tunes chosen are quite serviceable and had relatively unmemorable texts to begin with. But I have no desire to sing "new improved" words to "O Come All Ye Faithful" or to mouth platitudes from "The Little Prince" set to the glorious folk melody "Wailie, Wailie."

Perhaps we simply need to be reminded of the glory of singing together and the meaning that can evoke. The Dutch poet Huub Oosterhuis, who has collaborated with Huijbers on many liturgical pieces, says it well:

> To sing contagiously; catching fire from each other.
> This is what I want to see and to experience. . . .
>
> To sing what you are; what you live, and have lived so long, laboring, taciturn, dazed, lonely, not knowing, jabbering, stammering; your town, your hands, your questions, your wife, your friends, your voice, your past, your future-here-and now. . . .
>
> Training in waiting, humming, listening, being silent.
> Training in imagination, feeling, ecstasy.
> By doing, to become greater than you. . . .
>
> I believe in believing songs, which contain words that can only be sung, which are defenseless as only songs can be, which know what cannot be known.
> That is what I want to see and to experience. . . .

("At Times I See," pp. 112–113)

HYMNS IN HISTORY

Dr. Alice Parker

Composer and conductor, New York, N.Y.

Who were the first people who sang? Who were the first people who sang in worship? What brought people to sing in the first place? Of course we have no written records; all we do know, however, is that there is no aboriginal culture that has ever been found on the Earth that did not worship and that did not include song with its worship.

So the song is built in, and surely the first songs all grew out of "life situations." One of the most natural songs has to be that of a mother crooning to her baby. What are the musical elements? Certainly not perfection of performance; and you don't even have to have a song. What you have is a will to communicate, in this case, communicating not only comfort, gentleness and sleep, but also the actual vibration of the chest, which is transmitted to the child.

Communication is at the root of all song, and not so much communication with nature or with God, but with humans. When we have established communication with humans, then we can take it the step further, to a communication with God. But unless we establish that kind of touch — the literal touch between the throat that inaugurates the sound and the ear that receives it — we are not doing music.

There's no such thing as abstract music. There's no such thing as the note "A" — which piece is it in? what note comes before it? what after? what word are you singing? There's no such thing as 4/4. What kind of a 4/4? We get much too much concerned with the fine points of theory and not nearly enough concerned with the infinite possibilities of communication. Somehow the whole idea of what is important in music totally turns over when you look at it this way: correct notes are not important, correct rhythms are not important, tempo according to the metronome marking is not important—they are all absolutely necessary *if* the spirit is there that communicates; but they are *nothing* without that communicating spirit.

So life situations are called for in song—the life cycle, children's songs, games, dances, young people's love songs, courting songs, all kinds of work songs, anything that calls forth a rhythm; songs of mourning; certainly any human emotion can call forth song. And the first songs *had* to come this way. They were not something printed on a piece of paper that someone learned. They came from inside.

Music should have that fundamental point of departure. We should never sing a hymn without thinking to ourselves first, "What are we trying to communicate?" Very often it's not what the words are communicating. The words are marvelous, but if the words get in the way of the music, we shouldn't sing them with the music. The words can mean many different things; the words can be read at many different tempos and in many different tones of voice, but if we color the music to go with the words, we lose the music: if we're singing a march, it must march, and if we're singing a love song, it must sound like a love song.

If we move rapidly down the millenia, we see the Church developing—our Western Church, the Roman Church—basing traditions on music that had existed for centuries before. We see the chant developing, and the liturgy developing to a height of sophistication and beauty in the Middle Ages that is a rare and precious heritage for all of us.

The traditions develop, and we're all sharing in this age-old process of worship. Whenever we stop time and look at a moment in human history, we find different forces at work, just like the ones that are at work now. There are people who want to uphold the traditional way of doing things; there are those who want new things. There are people who are willing to sing and love to sing; there are those who don't want to sing. There are people who are all for instrumental music in the Church and there are people who want only singing. These are human problems that have existed in all societies and all ages, and they are certainly not limited to Catholic church musicians. Exactly the same problems are shared in the Protestant churches all over this country.

The thing that those of us who really believe in music have is a faith in the power of sound to communicate something that words cannot. Music is meant to move people. It should move people to tears, to laughter, or joy, or serenity. If it doesn't move people—if it is "only service music," or "only hymns"—then we're denying it the possibility of movement. We should never sing a note without first establishing the communication. The hymnal, any hymnal, is a marvelous tool for this. But if we accept a hymn at face value—that is, if we think that performing it the way it is on the page, singing the right notes and the right rhythms and the right words, is making music—we are in sad error. There is no guarantee written into the page that the performance of what is on it will automatically confer blessing.

We must bring 50 percent to the page. Composers are very aware of this. What I put on the page is meaningless to someone who doesn't know the style of the music that I'm writing. Someone who knows it can say, "Oh, I know just how that should sound." But for someone else to pick it up and try to do exactly what's on the page can be agony for the composer.

There really is no such thing as dull music. No composer ever sat down at his desk and said, "Well, today I'm going to write a really dull piece"! There is always *some* spark! Of course, there are all kinds of composers and all varieties of pieces; some are much more successful than others. As a composer, you really have very little control over that—you write the best you can that day. But somehow there's a spark, and unless you recapture that spark, you haven't done the piece; you haven't found what it is that the piece is communicating.

The fundamental truth is that music is sound, not marks on the page. Consider the phrase, "sound in the room." What kind of sound can we make, right now, in this room, just us? If another person comes in, or one of us should leave, it would be different. If it were this afternoon or tonight or yesterday, it would be different. What can we do *right now* that all of us participate in, that will make music that is a worthy offering?

We lose spontaneity by perceiving a huge difference between a rehearsal and a performance, or a rehearsal and a service; we wish we had a choir like the one in a larger town; we wish we had music or people who could sightread or instruments or something; and in longing for something else, we don't take advantage of what we have. Where two or three are gathered together, music can be made *if* this goal of communication is first.

When I began teaching choral arranging, I had to unlearn much of what I had learned in conservatory. I had to come to a fundamental relationship with melody, just as I imagine those earliest humans created song out of their own throats, and out of their own needs. What they sang was melody—not harmony, not counterpoint, not anthems—it was pure melody.

One basic realization was that you have to respect any melody that lasts. It won't last if it is wrong. If it's dull to you, it's probably because you're not doing it right! Any melody that survives its own immediate moment deserves respect.

The other basic thing I learned is a way of looking at a whole collection of melodies, as you would see them in a folk song collection or a hymnal, and screening out all of the unnecessary data—the tempo markings, the text, the harmonization—and looking only at the melody. As I do so, I am singing in my throat. I literally feel those muscles moving, and I feel, in every fiber of my body, the ones that lead to sound, the ones I want to work with.

It is useful to separate out the elements of the tunes so that you see them in their simplest form. The words can be isolated, and read like a poem. All the texts in the hymnals are poems. How often do you read them as poems? think about their structure, their meaning? the difference in tone from one verse to another? where the climax point is in the whole text? Remember that our contemporary hymnals are very chary of verses. Most hymn texts have far more verses—people used to sing much more lengthily than we do now. In fact, a popular kind of hymn a century ago was the alphabet hymn, in which there were 26 verses, each one beginning with a successive letter of the alphabet!

Next separate out the tune, too. If you write out a chant with one phrase on a line, you can see by glancing at it the relative structure of the musical phrases—for instance, some are longer than others. There are basically two kinds of notes, long and short. When chant gets written with stems on the notes, people tend to read them as quarter notes, which of course doesn't apply. We are in a complete historical inversion when we read chant metrically and when we harmonize it. Meter and harmony both came way after the time when chant was sung.

We should think back, as well as we can, not only to how it was sung when it was at its height of beauty, but to the individual throat. How does the individual singer relate to the tune? One of the first things that you're going to have to find out is how you're going to be able to breathe. This is enormously fundamental. We cannot sing without breathing. How are we using our breath on this tune? Do you want to breathe at the end of every phrase? Do you split a phrase for breath? Are there two phrases in one breath? You get your tempo, most of the time, from breath.

Also realize that many of the difficulties we encounter when we write a melody down are *page* problems, not singing problems. For instance, say a piece starts on E^b. E^b is an abstraction. If I take my pitch from the Lord and do whatever comes to my throat, I know that whatever pitch I take now I will be able to sustain through the whole piece. I will not do it at anyone else's convenience. There is no reason why this piece must always be sung in E^b just because it is written that way.

Chant is based on the words. There is no such thing as notating the rhythm of chant. The rhythm of chant is the rhythm of the words, and it is the rhythm of the words when they are read beautifully, not when they are just mumbled.

When we sing, we often lose the difference between accented and unaccented syllables. They all come out the same. For instance, take the word begotten. We do not speak it "bee-got-ten," but somehow we think that's the way to sing it. Listen for the wonderful subtle differences in spoken language and take that as the basis for the sung version — rather than a dull, undifferentiated reading. It can be like ocean waves — you're cresting constantly, you hesitate a moment at the top, and then you slide down with a wonderful swoop into the next one; don't step down in stairs!

We don't have to sing in perfect unison. Imagine singing in a medieval cathedral, where there's no conductor standing in the middle of the room. The important thing is the relationship of the individual singer to what s/he is singing. The acoustics — and that wonderful reverberation time — cancel out any attempts to do something exactly together. It doesn't matter. What matters is surrendering ourselves to those waves of sound.

Sing loaded syllables. Sing punctuation: never slide over a comma. Make different kinds of stops for commas than for semicolons. This kind of music follows natural laws. The highest note is the loudest one; float down to the lowest note, which should be the softest — very gentle. Be constantly aware of where you are on this scale.

Someone said, "We need to bring a sense of awe, of mystery, back into our services." And this is exactly what this music does, better than any other music that has ever lived. It exactly filled its function in those medieval churches — reflecting that atmosphere of awe and mystery, which the Mass is about.

If we turn the page of history to the Renaissance, we come to the beginning of the Protestant tradition. To recapitulate very briefly, we have almost an opposite set of needs and functions to be fulfilled now. Instead of the Mass in Latin, we have an enormous demand for the Psalms, and the whole service, in the language of the people. Instead of a beautifully established liturgy, we have people beginning all over again. Instead of chants, which were learned over lifetimes and developed over centuries, we have the idea of congregational song as one of the most potent teaching tools for doctrine that could possibly be imagined.

One of the reasons that the Protestant faith and its different denominations spread so quickly was that the first thing to be translated was the Book of Psalms, in meter. Literally hundreds of these songbooks arose. Everyone translated the Psalms. There are incredibly rich settings, in French, German, English, Scottish, all the different dialects you can imagine and all the different points of view toward the Psalms. Every new setting literally teaches something new about a Psalm. It holds the word meanings up as if a prism, with the light striking the prism from a different point. The many different kinds of translations should be historically researched, and brought out to be of use to us all.

There is no such thing as rhythmic music that is not somehow related to the movement of a human body—not necessarily that of a trained dancer—just as there is no such thing as 4/4. Such an abstraction is very convenient for our use in music, but for performance, we need to think, "What kind of a dance is it?" In the Renaissance again, the notation on the page was often just a beginning point. You learned by ear. When you looked at the page, you said, "Oh, I remember how that should go," and there was never just one way, as there is just one way to sing the Bach B Minor *Mass* or the Beethoven *Missa Solemnis*. It was a very different relationship with the page, much looser. When we rediscover that looseness, it leads us into lovely performance possibilities.

Think of the period of the Renaissance in music. What are the characteristic sounds? Instrumental sounds—recorders, harpsichords, viols, lutes—those soft instruments that go *bing*! There's a very clear beginning to the sound, then a quick decay. The music was apt to move lightly. You can't imagine a madrigal done in Brahms' style—it just doesn't work. We need to make a huge change in the way we use our throat muscles in order to sing a madrigal properly.

When music begins to say, "Oh, do me again!," it begins to have personality. Until we have found that kind of sound, we haven't begun to realize what is on the page. That's the difference between dull and living music. It must charm the ear—that's what sound is for.

Part of the trouble with our modern, comfortable hymnals is that we don't have to think when we use them. Hymnals weren't always so comfortable. In the old days, people's oral memories were much better: the hymnals had vast quantities of texts in the front, with a few tunes in the back that *everybody knew*.

One way to vary a melody is by changing the rhythmic mode, for instance from 4/4 to 3/4. You will find that the music communicates something totally different. Again, you have to ignore what you know about spoken rhythm. A delightful way to vary the rhythm is to use a basic quarter-note pulse and lengthen the *loaded* syllables. Make them half notes. Also, take a beat to breathe at the end of every line. (Without a trained voice, I like to breathe often!) It's a beautiful way to preach the text. It comes forth with the most wonderful meaning. You are underlining all of the grammatical and semantic aspects of the text when you sing it that way.

Moving briefly to the folk hymn, one of the first things you want to know (and this goes for any melody) is whether you are dealing with a pitch piece or a rhythm piece. If it's a pitch piece, you have time to breathe—you can add an extra beat for breath without disturbing anything; you can hold a high note; you can linger over a loaded syllable. You don't have to hold strictly to the 4/4.

When it's a rhythm piece, nothing should get in the way of the rhythm. You have to keep imaginary dancers in your mind and realize that if you add an extra beat, your dancers will vanish.

Any time you find a pentatonic tune in a folk hymn, treat it as pure gold. Often they are wrongly harmonized in a regular, major or minor kind of succession. It is wrong because notes are used in the harmonization that are not in the melody. This is not to say that you must stick only to the notes in the melody, but you get a perfectly gorgeous harmony that grows totally out of the music if you restrict yourself to the pentatonic scale.

Try doing it in a canon. You will find that your rhythm will improve because you have to sing your part stronger. You'll have to grab on to it and keep ahold of it; you can't just relax into it. The canon mode *forces* the rhythm to come better.

It's easy enough to do countless numbers of parts in a canon, even without previous warning. What you end up with is the sound that was sung in those country churches in the Virginia hills—not neatly read out of a book, with someone frowning and calling out the mistakes—but a free kind of sound.

The nicest thing about this way of looking at music is that you know that you can't do one bit of it by yourself, but that we can all combine to do it superbly. Try it!

LTP RESOURCES

THE LITURGY DOCUMENTS. The most important statements on liturgy from Rome and the U.S. bishops in one volume. $6.45

LITURGY WITH STYLE AND GRACE. Short essays on the basic elements of liturgy and liturgy planning. $6.45

CELEBRATING LITURGY. *The* book to assist lectors, liturgy planners, homilists, and musicians week in, week out through the whole liturgical year. $6.50

AT HOME WITH THE WORD. Three Sunday readings on one page and a number of thought-provoking questions based on the readings on the facing page. $1.75

CANTORS AND LEADERS OF SONG. Three 60-minute cassettes for cantor training, recorded live at cantor workshops in Chicago. $19.95

GOAL-SETTING FOR LITURGY TEAMS. Ideas and exercises to help new, established and faltering teams to move ahead. $4.50

EVENING PRAYER IN THE PARISH. Explains the tradition of Christian prayer and offers a careful description of the ritual with practical suggestions for introducing evening prayer in a parish. $2.40 **LEADER'S BOOK** $6.50. **EVENING PRAYER CARD** 10 for $1.50.

HANDBOOK FOR CHURCH MUSIC FOR WEDDINGS. Brief introductions and extended listings of appropriate church music for the various ritual moments within the wedding liturgy. $1.25

THE WEDDING MUSIC CASSETTE. 60-minute cassette of 29 different musical selections for various moments of the wedding liturgy. $8.00

NPM RESOURCES

PASTORAL MUSIC, journal of the National Association of Pastoral Musicians. Excellent articles concerning good musical liturgy, with regular features for musicians and clergy. Published six times a year, $18.00 subscription rate per year.

TO GIVE THANKS AND PRAISE. General Instruction of the Roman Missal, With Commentary for Musicians and Clergy. By Ralph Keifer. Contains the *General Instruction* in its entirety, plus Keifer's clear commentary which focuses on the needs of pastoral musicians and clergy who minister at the parish level. (165 pp.) $4.95

MUSIC IN CATHOLIC WORSHIP: THE NPM COMMENTARY (Revised Edition, edited by Virgil C. Funk.) Includes both the document, "Music in Catholic Worship," and thorough commentary. Gives you a section by section look at the document. (178 pp.) $5.95

WHY SING? TOWARD A THEOLOGY OF CATHOLIC CHURCH MUSIC. By Miriam Therese Winter. Weaves together the development of Vatican II documents and 20th century church legislation. Its select bibliography contains over 2100 titles. (352 pp.) $11.95

INTRODUCING DANCE IN CHRISTIAN WORSHIP. By Ronald Gagne, Thomas Kane, and Robert VerEecke. With Introduction by Carla DeSola, Annotated Bibliography by Gloria Weyman. Presents history, models, and examples of dance in liturgy. How to dance. Why to dance. (112 pp., 49 photographs) $7.95

Available from your bookstore or:
The Pastoral Press
225 Sheridan Street, NW
Washington, DC 20011
(202) 723-5800

The Pastoral Press
A Division of the National Association of Pastoral Musicians